DECISION MAKING IN PUBLIC SECTOR

WITH CASE STUDIES

I K ACHPLANI

INDIA • SINGAPORE • MALAYSIA

Notion Press

No. 8, 3rd Cross Street,
CIT Colony, Mylapore,
Chennai, Tamil Nadu – 600 004

First Published by Notion Press 2020
Copyright © I K Achplani 2020
All Rights Reserved.

ISBN 978-1-63669-671-3

This book has been published with all efforts taken to make the material error-free after the consent of the author. However, the author and the publisher do not assume and hereby disclaim any liability to any party for any loss, damage, or disruption caused by errors or omissions, whether such errors or omissions result from negligence, accident, or any other cause.

While every effort has been made to avoid any mistake or omission, this publication is being sold on the condition and understanding that neither the author nor the publishers or printers would be liable in any manner to any person by reason of any mistake or omission in this publication or for any action taken or omitted to be taken or advice rendered or accepted on the basis of this work. For any defect in printing or binding the publishers will be liable only to replace the defective copy by another copy of this work then available.

Dedication

This book is affectionately
Dedicated to our beloved
Kunal

Love you beta!!!

Contents

Foreword *9*
Preface *11*

1. Introduction to Decision-Making 15
2. Essentials of Decision Making 19
3. Dilemma in Decision Making 23
   - Spending Others' Money 23
4. Transparency in Decision Making 29
5. Effective Business Communication 33
6. Tenets of Public Procurement 39
7. Enablers for Effective Decision Making 45
   - Systems and Procedures 48
8. Negotiation – Commercial Issues 51

9. **Scanning of Decisions in PSEs** 59
    - Vigilance Functions 60
        - Preventive Vigilance 61
        - Predictive Vigilance 61
        - Punitive Vigilance 61
    - Comptroller and Auditor General of India (CAG) 64
    - Central Vigilance Commission (CVC) 67
    - Chief Technical Examiners' Organization (CTEO) 69
    - Integrity Pact (IP) 69
    - CVC's Jurisdiction 73
    - Central Bureau of Investigation (CBI) 73
10. **Decision-Making Process** 75
11. **Philosophy of Decision Making** 79
    - The Utilitarian Approach 80
    - The Rights Approach 80
    - The Fairness or Justice Approach 81
    - The Common-Good Approach 81
    - The Virtue Approach 82
    - Ethical Problem Solving 82

    Exercise on Ethical Problem Solving 85
12. **Factors Influencing Decision Making** 89
    - Perception 90
    - Intuitive Decision-Making Process 93
    - Organizational Issues 94
    - Environment 97

    MCQ – Factors Affecting Decision Making 101
13. **Project Contracts and Common Allegations** 107

14. **Indenting/Tendering & Common Irregularities** 111
    - Justification of Quantity 112
    - Eligibility Criteria 112
    - Specifications 113
    - Preparation of Estimate 113
    - Acceptance/Rejection Criteria 114
    - Tendering 114
15. **Decision Making – Case Studies** 119
    - Case No. 1–30 120-178
16. **Decision Making in PSE – MCQ Exercise** 181

Foreword

The success of any Organization – be it a Private or a Public Sector Enterprise (PSE) depends to a greater degree on the strength of its decision making structure. A timely and well considered decision is like the spark that set the machinery into motion. Thus, the importance of decision making needs to be appreciated and should not be undermined at any stage. However, in case of PSE, the problem is compounded as decision making is found wanting practically at all levels.

Most of the PSEs were set up in the 1960s and 70s with an aim to cater the needs of independent India which was then in its infancy stage. While these Companies proved to be the knights in shining armour and played their role to perfection in building the modern India, of late they seem to have lost their way.

With the opening up of the economy, the intensifying competition from the private sector as well as global MNCs has taken a toll on these government owned corporate. With the passing of times, the technology, the methods and other resources employed by these PSEs have become outdated. Some of the PSEs have tried to reinvent their techniques yet find themselves lagging the peers from private sector. The major reason for the same has been inability to keep pace with the changing times which in itself emanates from the slow and poor recording of reason for deviation, if any, is also cited as one of the important factors responsible for delay. This could also be a result of the fear of vigilance or audit, inadequate data/MIS, no proper appraisals/analysis, etc.

In this regard, the book on "Decision Making in Public Sector" by Shri I K Achplani can prove to be guide that everyone is on a look out for Shri Achplani has gathered varied experience during his service career so far and has quite beautifully penned down his thoughts, ideas and suggestions in the form of a book. Not only will it help the people in decision making positions today but will also make a good read even for those aspring to reach these positions of decision making in future.

I wish him all the best for the success of his book. I hope it is read and liked by one and all.

Sd/-
Anil Kumar Chaudhary,
Chairman
Steel Authority of India Limited

Preface

The canons of Procurement are to procure work, material/services of the specified quality within the specified time at the most competitive prices. However, when it comes to public procurement, in addition to the above, the decision-maker has to ensure that the procurement is done in a ***fair, just, and transparent manner.***

Although, there is a difference of only two words between private procurement and public procurement i.e. Fairness and Transparency compliance of these two requirements results in increased cost of procurement in Public Sector Enterprises, which I have termed as **"EFFORT COST"** and the magnitude of this cost is enormous.

During my around four decades stint in a Maharatna PSE, I got the opportunity to work in various managerial posts including in Finance, Marketing, Corporate Vigilance, Internal Audit, and finally as a Senior Faculty in the area of Commercial Acumen and Decision making. I have also visited many other public sector enterprises as guest faculty and it's my strong belief that most of the PSE executives are intelligent, mature, knowledgeable, honest, and dedicated. Yet, when it comes to decision making, they are afraid of taking decisions due to fear of being questioned by the various investigating/audit agencies on the veracity/correctness of the decisions taken by them.

It's a fact that risks are an integral part of complex, high-stakes decisions, and decision-makers are faced with the unavoidable tasks of assessing risks and forming risk preferences. The risks are of two types **"Real Risks"** and **"Perceived Risks"**. While executives are capable of assessing real risks in a decision being taken and mitigate them, it's their fear of "Perceived risks" which delays the decision-making in the Public Sector.

The genuineness of a decision is judged based on the available facts and circumstances prevailing at the time of decision making. This book is an effort to take out the fear of "perceived risks" from the mind of decision-makers and to give them the confidence in performing their jobs to the best of their ability. Right intent is the key to decision making and should be made visible in the records. I love the following quote on "learning" by Confucius:

> *"By three methods we may learn wisdom; first, by reflection, which is noblest; second, by imitation, which is easiest; and third by experience, which is the bitterest."*

If you will try to learn from your own mistakes, although it will be great learning but there is every possibility that vigilance and audit may not spare you for the omissions done.

Through various case-studies included in this book and decision-making exercises, readers will learn to make logical and rational decisions under the given situation/circumstances.

Faster, rational, and effective decision-making shall help the companies to save wastage towards "Effort Costs" thus making them more prosperous, competitive, and sustainable to withstand global competition.

I express my sincere gratitude to my first boss respected Shri S K Roongta, ex-CMD, SAIL who advised me at a very young age that ***"Knowledge is Power* – acquire it from wherever available"**. That's what

I am doing to date and this book is a compilation of my knowledge and experience gained during my professional journey. Thank you, sir!!!

I am grateful to respected Shri Anil Kumar Chaudhary, Chairman, SAIL, all my seniors & colleagues in SAIL, friends, and family members for their whole-hearted help, support, and guidance in my endeavor to write this book and special thanks to my dear friend Mr. Samir Swarup, Chief General Manager, SAIL for his invaluable suggestions and editing of the book.

– Inder Kumar Achplani
achpalani@gmail.com

CHAPTER 01

Introduction to Decision-Making

"Wherever you see a successful business, someone once made a courageous decision"

– Peter Drucker

Decision making is a difficult task. One has to choose the best alternative from amongst many possible alternatives to solve the problem and getting the desired/envisaged result on its implementation! This is the biggest challenge in decision making. You take a decision weighing all possible alternatives, presuming and assuming many things, considering both real as well as perceived risks involved in the decision, and finally selects the best alternative basing it on sound rationale/logic as it appears to you. All this is theoretical because the outcome shall be visible only after implementing the decision. That's the biggest challenge in decision making. This becomes more challenging when you are required to make decisions on someone else's behalf as we are doing in the public sector when spending public money.

An example given by the Director (Finance) of a Public Sector Undertaking during interaction with the senior executives of his Company triggered the thought in me to write a book on decision making in the Public Sector.

During interaction with the participants, he recalled an incident when a supplier who charged Rs. 900 crores for supply/erection/commissioning of a Mill from the private sector company, emerged as the Lowest Bidder for the same mill with the same scope of work at Rs. 1100 crores in a Public Sector company.

Can you think of any valid reason for paying Rs. 200 crores more for the same job or did the PSU pay this extra amount just because it is public money?

The reason is clear, PSU paid this money towards his "Efforts cost". The supplier added Rs. 200 crores towards his efforts cost while quoting for the public sector because he knew that he had to incur this extra amount of Rs. 200 crores while executing the job for a PSU. Why and How? Here, I am not hinting at any corruption.

In accounting, the cost is usually a monetary valuation of efforts, material, resources, time, and utilities consumed. Theoretically "effort" means processing time but generally while evaluating the project cost, suppliers tend to add many other costs while computing the total cost which incidentally varies from client to client.

In the case of a Public Sector, the first effort cost is towards the tender processing time by the buyer i.e. the gap between the time when the supplier will submit the tender and the time when the tender shall be finalized. Inflation is a continuous phenomenon, it will keep rising although the supplier has to quote the rates as on the day he is submitting the tender. Therefore, he has to make provision for a rise in prices from tender finalization until the successful execution of the job. Can you think of any project tender in your company that was awarded in time? Most probably, the answer shall be no as the techno-commercial evaluation of a complex tender is in itself is a time-consuming activity, and decisions are required to be taken at many levels.

During execution also, the supplier will face many hurdles especially if it is a Brownfield project. First, he will not get the site in time, even when handed-over to him; it may require minor changes in the pre-approved drawings/designs due to bottlenecks that could not be foreseen by the tenderer. Approval for these drawing/design changes will also take a very long time due to administrative reasons and hierarchy. This will make the Supplier/Contractor incur losses due to idling of his contract workers, non-utilization of his material, and machines that would already have reached the site resulting in blocking of his working capital.

Further, during the processing of his running bills, bills will be sent from table to table, seeking clarifications/justifications, etc. as no executive will like to decide at his end on issues not falling within his jurisdiction. Although it is the internal set-up of a PSU and the procedures/guidelines framed by them stipulate thorough scrutiny of the bills, the fact remains that sufferer in this case also shall be the supplier who has to arrange working capital from his end to keep project work running thus incurring the extra burden of the interest cost. There can be many other issues beyond these examples. However, all these issues result in higher total costs for the supplier. Thus, keeping his margin the same, he is bound to quote a higher price against a PSU tender.

If you will try to find out the reasons for the delay, take my words, the biggest reason emerging out shall be the delay in decision making that too mainly for reasons attributable to "perceived risks" of decision-maker.

As per the definition given in the Business Directory, "Decision Making is a process of selecting a logical choice from the available options when trying to make a good decision". The decision-maker must weigh the positives and negatives of each option and consider all the alternatives. For effective decision making, a person must be able to forecast the outcome of each option as well, and based on all these items, determine which option is the best for that particular situation.

Although it is a very concise and apt definition of decision making but weighing the positives and negatives of each alternative while making a decision is a cumbersome and risky process especially when we are spending other's money i.e. public money. If we have to make Public Sector Undertakings sustainable, profitable and competitive in the era of global competition, the first thing is to enhance/improve the decision-making capabilities of public sector executives to enable them to take faster, logical and effective decisions in a time-bound manner.

With over forty years of experience in the public sector and after working in various managerial positions including my stint in the Corporate Vigilance Department and Internal Audit Department of a Maharatna PSU, I can vouch that most of the public sector executives are fair, honest, sincere, and hardworking and dedicated but they are very emotional. What do I mean by emotional, you will be able to appreciate only when you will try to make decisions under the situations enumerated in various case-lets given in the book.

Public Sector executives are mature, intelligent, and experienced enough to foresee the actual risks in the decision they are going to take but they are always afraid of "Perceived risks" which delays the decision making. These perceived risks take away their courage thus resulting in avoidable delays in decision making.

This book will guide you to take effective decisions in a time-bound manner without fear of third agencies who may always be scrutinizing your decisions i.e. how to get rid of your perceived risks?

Faster, rational and effective decision making shall help your Company save the outflow of funds which are being charged by the vendors/contractors/suppliers from the PSEs in the name of "Efforts Costs" thus making your Organization more prosperous, competitive, and sustainable to withstand global competition.

CHAPTER 02

Essentials of Decision Making

"You can't make decisions based on fear and the possibility of what might happen."

— Michelle Obama

Let's try to understand the definition of decision making by trying to decide the following case:

"Suppose you have gone to market with your wife and 8-9-year-old son for purchasing furniture for your newly built home. As you have to look for items that meet your requirements, aesthetics, color, etc. you search for the same at various shops. Your son is getting bored and disturbing you. You bought a few pretty big chocolates and gave one to your son to pacify him. Immediately after eating the first chocolate, he starts crying for the second one. Will you give him the second chocolate?"

Simple isn't it. Then take a decision!

I don't know, whether you have decided to give second chocolate to your son or not but I am pretty sure, whatever your decision is, it's an outcome of the following 4 "C"

- Courage
- Conviction/confidence

- Competence
- Commitment/will

In the above case, to say yes or no to your son for the second chocolate, it requires "courage". How?

You have the second chocolate, you can easily give your son another one as he is crying for the same but you are worried about his health especially dental issues. Now the decision-making is within your emotional issues i.e. although you don't want your child to cry, fundamental/rational issues concerning the health of your child are stopping you from giving him the second chocolate. You want your son to always stay fit and healthy thus you will say "no" ignoring his cry, which requires courage. It may also happen that you will give him the chocolate as you cannot see your son crying because your knowledge says that one more chocolate is not going to affect his health and you want him to be happy, again it requires courage.

The next question is from where you will get this courage to say "Yes" or "No"?

This yes or no will be the outcome of your "conviction" in either case i.e. if you are convinced that eating more chocolates at a time may damage his teeth and may lead to other health issues and you don't want to take that risk, you will say 'NO' to your child.

The other possibility can be that you are confident that one more chocolate is not going to harm him. Moreover, you always love to see your kid happy; you will convince yourself that his smile is more precious than anything else. This thought will immediately convince you that eating one more chocolate is not going to be that harmful to your child as compared to keep him crying and you may take a decision to give him the second chocolate.

Again, the question is from where this "confidence" will come?

This conviction or confidence will come in you to say yes or no, only if you know the subject i.e. how much chocolates can a child may consume in a day or say continuously without damaging his teeth and health and other consequences of giving or not giving the chocolate. Besides this, how to handle emotional conflict, etc. i.e. if you have the knowledge and competency in the area where you are required to take the decision, decision making will be easy, correct, and logical. The final yes or no in the instant case is the outcome of your "competency" and, believe me, knowing or unknowingly it has influenced your decision-making process.

What's the role of "commitment" in decision making in the above case?

There is a very big role of commitment in decision making e.g. in this case, let's assume, you are neither in the mood to give him another chocolate as you are concerned about his health nor you want to say no to your child as he is already crying and you are not able to pacify him. You have a very soft and easy option always available to you. You may redirect him to your wife, stating that first take permission of your mother and if she agrees, I will give you the second chocolate.

It simply means you are not "committed" to solve the problem or you lack the will to make a decision and face the consequences of decision making. That's what generally happens in the public sector especially when we are required to decide on critical matters where stakes are high! We tend to take advice from all the possible sources to ensure that the decision taken by us is the most effective decision concerning safety which results in delay in decision making and at times, inordinate delays!

Theoretically, in simplest terms, decision making is the study of identifying and choosing alternatives based on the values and preferences of the decision-maker. Making a decision implies that there are choices to be considered. In such a case, the decision-maker has to choose the:-

1. Alternative that has the highest probability of success or effectiveness.
2. Alternative that best fits with goals, desires, lifestyle, values, etc.
3. Alternative that is most ethical.

In the public sector, one most important attribute of decision making is that the decision should not only be fair, transparent, and rational but must also appear fair, transparent, and rational. This, in my opinion, is the biggest inhibitor in decision making for a public sector executive.

"Whether decision making is easy or difficult in public sector enterprises vis-à-vis decision making in a private sector enterprise?"

Please take a pause and decide on your answer, before we deliberate on the issue. I don't know what will be your reply, but most probably the reply shall be that "it is difficult to make decisions in the public sector".

This perception of mine is based on the replies received by me during my interactions with hundreds of PSE executives, right from entry-level to the senior-most level. Many told it is difficult, few told very difficultly, most of them told it's risky as you are always under the scanner and many told it is a time consuming and cumbersome exercise as you have to get your decision vetted/approved at various levels, etc.

Although there shall always be a difference between decision making in the public sector vis-à-vis decision making in the private sector because of mainly one major reason, which you will be able to appreciate after going through this small story and replying to the questions thereafter.

CHAPTER 03

Dilemma in Decision Making

"Have the courage of your convictions once you have made a decision."
— Walter Schloss

Spending Others' Money

Ram and Shyam are working in the same company, the same department for the last 10 years and they are family friends also as they live on the ground floor and the first floor of the same apartment block. In the last 10 years of their friendship, they have developed a lot of trust in each other.

One day evening, Ram who is on the first floor of the apartment, came down to go to the main market to buy certain household items. He met Shyam in the compound who inquired from Ram as to where he is going? Ram replied that he is going to the Main Market. Shyam asked him whether he could do a small favor and buy one particular item from the main market for him.

What will be the reply to Ram? The obvious reply shall be a big "YES" as I have told you that they are very good friends. Shyam then handed over an Rs. 100 note to Ram saying that the item may cost within Rs. 100 as he had last purchased it at Rs. 80/-. Ram said nothing to worry; I will get the item for you and proceeded to the market.

Ram reached the market and thought of buying Ram's item first and then does his purchasing. He went to the first shop where such items may be available and enquired about the required stuff. Item was available and the shopkeeper revealed its price as Rs. 100/-. Ram requested him to charge the correct price but shop keeper confidently told it is his best price and item may not be available at a lesser price in the entire market. Ram took a 'U' turn murmuring that this shopkeeper is trying to rob him. He proceeded further and after about 25-30 steps found another shop where the item could be available and enquired about the item. Item was available and shop keeper asked Rs. 95/- as its price. Ram pleaded to reduce the price but the shopkeeper asked him that this is the best price he has offered and Ram will not get it at a lesser price anywhere in the market, the same words as were told by the first shop keeper. Ram came out of the shop to try his luck at the third shop perceiving that it can get a reduction of Rs. 5/- by walking 25-30 steps; he must walk down a little further to get the most competitive price. He found another shop where the item could be available and fortunately the item was available in the shop. Shopkeeper, however, asked Rs. 95/- as its price. Now, Ram was confused, he started bargaining with the shopkeeper and used all his negotiation skills. Shop keeper ultimately agreed to charge Rs. 90/- as the final price and requested Ram to decide early as other customers were waiting in the shop.

Ram purchased the item at Rs. 90/- and took the cash-memo for the item purchased. Thereafter, he did his purchasing and after coming back to his apartment, he first knocked at the door of Shyam and handed over to him, the item, balance change, and cash-memo. He said sorry to Shyam that he could not buy it at Rs. 80/-. Shyam thanked Ram ten times for his help and threw the cash-memo in the dust-bin stating that he bought the item around ten months back and he was apprehensive that it may cost more than Rs. 100/- whereas he had given Rs. 100/- only.

Here is a question for you, why did Ram take the cash-memo? Please keep in mind that they are very good friends and Shyam had not bothered to look at the cash-memo and threw it in the dust-bin. While replying to the question, try to recollect from your memory, how many times you took the cash-memo for such petty purchases.

Park the question in your mind and read the under-mentioned story with a fresh mind and no backlogs.

In the same story, there is a small change. The story remains the same till Ram came downstairs to go to the market and the conversation between Ram and Shyam. After that please forget the old story and read the new one.

Ram was in a great hurry as his wife asked him to get some stuff for the cake which she already started baking and wanted that item within 15-20 minutes otherwise all her efforts would go futile. We are all obedient husbands and Ram is one amongst us and we always try to keep our better halves happy. Ram immediately got ready and came downstairs to go to the market and get what his wife wanted and that too within the stipulated time.

However, when he met Shyam and talked to him, he could not say no to him because of their friendship and offered to do his work and proceeded to the market. He inquired about the item required by Shyam at the first shop and luckily it was available. Shop keeper asked him Rs. 100/- for the item and confidently told Ram that this is the cheapest rate and he will not get the item at a lesser price in the whole market. Because of the paucity of time, Ram got convinced and purchased the item and requested for cash-memo for the same, which the shop keeper gladly issued.

After purchasing the items for which he went to the market, he reached back home within time and first handed over the items to his wife and got compliments from her for the timely help. He was on cloud 9 when his wife said "you are the best husband in the world". Ram went downstairs and handed over the item to Shyam along with the cash-memo. He said sorry to Shyam as he could not get it at Rs. 80/-. Shyam thanked him ten times for the help provided and said that he purchased the item around ten months back and was worried that it may cost more than Rs. 100/- whereas he gave only one hundred rupee note for procuring the item. Shyam never bothered to look at the cash-memo and threw it in the dust bin.

Ram came back home, had dinner and cake, and went to bed for enjoying a sound sleep. But here, we are discussing the life of a public sector executive; many will always envy your happiness and keep trying to disturb your nights.

Someone complained that Ram has swindled Rs. 10/- in this purchase as this item is readily available at Rs. 90/- in the market. To substantiate his allegation, the complainant attached few cash memos for the item where the price charged was found mentioned as Rs. 90/- only.

Now, suppose you have been assigned the job to find out whether Ram is guilty or not in the second episode mentioned above. You have to investigate the case and give your recommendations.

The decision is in your hands and you are in an ethical dilemma as you know the background as to why Ram was in hurry on that particular day, but on the other hand, you are also aware that the item is available at Rs. 90/- as is evident from the cash memos attached by the complainant along with his complaint.

Take your time and decide whether in your opinion Ram is guilty "yes" or not guilty "no". My earnest request is not to proceed further with the reading until you make up your mind.

To help you in decision making, let me make it clear to you that if it comes to your mind that this purchase was made in an emergency, kindly recall that emergency was at Ram's end whereas the extra money spent was of Shyam i.e. you cannot put others to a loss for mitigating your emergency.

On the other hand, if it's coming to your mind that Ram is guilty, then what is the reason for your decision?

The only reason which may come to your mind is that the general practice of procurement is to explore the market, buy the item at the competitive rates, a bargain if the price asked is more than the estimated price, etc. and Ram has not taken these precautions while making procurement in the instant case, thus he is guilty.

Waiting for your reply…

Let's presume you are ready with the answer. Undoubtedly, your answer shall be either "yes" or "no".

Yes or no is your choice but please elaborate the basis on which you decided this yes i.e. guilty or no i.e. not guilty. Basis can be any written down procedure/guideline, customary or practice (even if you say it is customary of procurement, please think as to how many times you followed this practice for your purchase of this small value). Believe me, you will not be able to find any benchmark for your reply, thus, your decision is the outcome of your "perception". Perception is one biggest factor which affects our decision making; therefore, we have dealt with perception separately in this book.

This is a case between two friends who trust each other and the conclusion can't be made merely on the perception of an individual who is investigating the case as there is neither any written guideline nor established practice of procurement for such type of personal transactions. Hence, my question itself is ambiguous.

Further, the allegation was that Ram has swindled the money whereas in my story I mentioned that Ram bought the item at Rs. 100/- and brought cash-memo for the same also. Therefore, it can be at most a case of negligence, which is again difficult to substantiate in absence of any procedure/guideline.

Why so many rules/procedures and guidelines in the public sector?

When a public sector employee is entrusted with the responsibility of spending public money, he should be given some protection to protect himself from such complaints as you have seen in the above case. Thus, in the public sector, decision making is supported by so many rules, procedures, and guidelines. How they act as enablers in decision making, we shall deliberate through various case studies.

However, the answer to the first question is still pending i.e. why Ram took the cash memo for such a petty purchase. Your obvious answer will be that it was others' money that Ram spent and Ram wanted to maintain the trust which Shyam has in him and he wanted to maintain transparency in the transaction.

From the above story, it can be summarized that taking a decision on other's behalf and more specifically spending other's money is a challenging task. In the Public Sector, we spend public money and since the owner of the money is public in general, anybody is free to ask us as to how we have spent his money? It is, therefore, utmost necessary for all employees of the public sector to maintain fairness and transparency in their decision making

CHAPTER 04

Transparency in Decision Making

"Sunshine is the greatest disinfectant"
— N Vittal, former CVC

Every executive of the public sector would have heard this word or read it in rules, procedures, and guidelines several times that they should always maintain transparency in all their decisions. Before proceeding further, let's try and understand the meaning of transparency.

We inherit certain virtues from our parents, school, society, and get so much influenced by these virtues that they become our character e.g. fairness, honesty, sincerity, loyalty, etc. These virtues are valued by us and are therefore called values. However, values are individual beliefs i.e. values of two individuals may not necessarily be the same.

As values represent our character, values are important to us, and under any situation, we try to make decisions based on our values. My question to the participants is as under:

"Although values are important to an individual as they represent his character but while discharging duties and responsibilities as an employee of Public Sector undertaking, there is something more important than your values. What's that?"

I have got many answers and the most common reply is that we have to abide by rules, procedures, and guidelines while discharging our duties in the public sector. But that may be true in your personal life also. For example, you stop your vehicle at Red signal on the road, because you are a law-abiding citizen.

The other common reply I generally receive is that we have to be loyal to our organization, but it is again your value, as you may be loyal to your family, friends, relatives, etc.

Without spending time analyzing many such replies, let us go quickly to the answer which is quite straight and simple.

"It is more important to appear valuable while discharging our duties and responsibilities in a public sector than our values i.e. all our virtues like honesty, fairness, sincerity, loyalty, adherence to rules, procedures and guidelines, etc. should be visible from the records generated at the time of taking a decision".

Little confused! What does it mean? Go back to the above story of Ram and Shyam, you were convinced that Ram's conscience was clear and it was only the circumstances which forced him to spend Rs. 10/- extra. However, what happened next when you were asked to investigate the case! Many of you proved Ram "guilty" because there is evidence that the item was available at a cheaper price.

Now that's a challenge in public sector decision making!

Therefore, in the public sector, we keep so much written record for every decision taken to prove as and when required, that the decision taken was the most effective decision under the situation when it was taken. To substantiate the fact that how careful we are in our endeavor to appear fair and transparent; if we send an important email to our client/customer/contractor/vendor, etc. we take out a print and nicely keep it in our records for future reference. Are you not doing it?

In the public sector, you will be seen as 'fair' and 'transparent' only if your records will speak so. Now that's a challenge! You know you are an honest executive and you are making decisions in the best interest of your

Organization. Will it serve the purpose to prove your honesty and sincerity when required?

I am sorry, but the answer is a big "NO". You have to appear fair and honest through the records you are generating at the time of taking decisions. Believe me, it looks simple but a difficult task because you take a decision when you are convinced that what you are doing is correct and it's the most effective decision possible in the given situation and circumstances. However, the challenge is that these circumstances and the situation under which you took the particular decision are your perceptions and should be available on records as to why you had perceived that way.

Your integrity and devotion to duty shall be assessed by the third agencies i.e. CAG, CVC and CBI, etc. which we will deal with in detail a little later in this book. The investigating officer shall not be aware of the situation or the circumstances under which you took a particular decision; he can only perceive the situation as reflected through the records.

I remember, one of our senior bosses was always telling us to prepare a speaking note! I was at a loss as to what does it mean? Believe me, it was after my posting in the vigilance department that I was able to understand and appreciate the meaning of a speaking note.

We are experts in our domain area but when it comes to putting our mind on a piece of paper, it is a challenging task for many of us. The basic reason being is that we have not learned the skill of effective business communication. Let's try and understand the tenets of effective business communication.

CHAPTER 05

Effective Business Communication

"Don't communicate to be understood; rather, communicate so as not to be misunderstood."

– Dr. John Lund

While taking a decision e.g. initiating a proposal for procurement of a new heavy-duty electric motor for your plant, you struggle with a lot of questions, such as:-

1. Whether procurement is at all required?
2. Do you have other alternatives e.g. repair of the existing motor, using spare motor lying in the plant, etc.?
3. What exactly you want to buy?
4. How you want to buy i.e. single tender, limited tender, or open tender?
5. What will be the estimated cost and how it will be arrived at?
6. From where to obtain budgetary quotes, if it is a new procurement and how many budgetary quotations shall be required?
7. Whether suppliers shall be willing to give a budgetary quote?

8. How to finalize eligibility criteria so that you get what you want to get yet at the same time invite sufficient competition for the same?

9. If you go for the best quality procurement and make specifications accordingly, will it not be seen as favoring the particular supplier?

10. How to keep the specification/criteria specific yet generic to maximize competition?

This list can be endless but the fact remains that you try and find out replies to all the above questions while initiating a procurement proposal.

However, the challenge is that all these answers should be available on records whereas the proposals are generally initiated covering the issues that require approval. The obvious reason is that you initiate a proposal after a lot of deliberations with your colleagues/juniors/seniors and after satisfying yourself about all the facts relating to the decision, you initiate the proposal on the issues where approval from Competent Authority is required as per your procedures/guidelines.

Approving Authorities also approve the proposal as they are aware of the background of the case as they are from the same environment as you and normally you have discussed the matter with them before initiating the proposal.

During my Vigilance tenure, during investigation or inspection of files, decisions taken were many times perceived by me as probably the most effective decisions possible under the circumstances. However, the relevant information and facts were not available on record in the various files which could enable me to substantiate my perceptions with facts. It needs to be appreciated that perceptions need to be substantiated by facts in any investigation report. More so, as these reports are required to be put up before Chief Vigilance Officer who is an outsider, he will act upon written facts only.

Vigilance functions on **"Preponderance of Probability"** i.e. investigating officer is not required to prove the allegation right or wrong with proof beyond reasonable doubt but it is only his perception based on the information available from records only matters. Therefore, invariably the last line in any investigation report generally is as under:

"It appears from the examination of records and facts revealed during investigation that the allegations are unsubstantiated, without basis, etc. or it can be the allegations are substantiated…" which may happen if the answers to questions coming in the mind of investigating officers are not answered from the available records nor replied satisfactorily as any later submissions/clarification (s) may be treated as an afterthought.

We started with some questions relating to the initiation of the proposal. Similar questions will crop up in the mind of the auditor/investigator also in case of an inquiry. Thus, your proposals should be detailed enough to provide credible answers to future perceived queries. This would also assist your superiors, who are concurring or approving authorities, to take correct decisions. Further, have you ever considered that after your proposal is approved, files shall be kept in records for scrutiny of your decisions by the third agency?

These third agencies may not be from within your organization. They are neither aware of the subject nor the environment under which you work or take decisions. They have to perceive everything from the written records presented before them during scrutiny/investigation. Isn't it a big challenge? Therefore, to make your communication effective, ask yourself the following questions to give a clear picture to your readers. If you imagine yourself in your reader's position, you're more likely to be an effective communicator:

Who are my readers?

- What do they already know about the subject?
- What do they need to know?
- Will they understand technical terms?
- What information do they want?

- What do I want them to do?
- What interests or motivates them?
- What prejudices do they have?
- What worries or reassures them?
- What will persuade them to my view?
- What other arguments do I need to present?
- How are they likely to react to what I say?

To be an effective communicator, you have to understand the following 7 "Cs" of communication:

i. Concise

Use concise and straightforward language that gets the point across completely and in a manner that encourages efficient action.

ii. Complete

Plan your business communication carefully so you get all of the information to your recipient the first time.

iii. Conversational

It is important to present your information in a conversational tone that invites interaction, rather than a confrontational tone that can cause an argument. Effective communication presents the information in a manner that is not emotional but instead professional.

iv. Clear

When you present your information, be sure to do so in a clear voice that allows every word to be understood either written or verbal.

v. Considerate

When speaking to business associates or customers, always open the conversation to questions and clarifications. When you answer a question, be sure the answer is understood before moving on in the conversation. The same rule applies to written communication also.

vi. Confidence

Present your data with a clear and commanding tone that indicates that you know the subject and the information being presented is valuable.

vii. Check

Always check your data and facts before presenting them. Keep in mind that even if the smallest error is observed in the facts or figures, the reader may not trust you.

Even after writing thousands of letters and initiating numerous proposals, I have not yet finalized any letter/proposal in the first attempt. Write a letter/note and leave it for some time and then read it, I guarantee you will do a few corrections/value additions. Try it out and see the magic! Your communication will improve day by day.

To become an effective communicator, the 4 "Cs" we discussed in decision making are very much required in your communication also, which means:

- You must be committed to ensuring that your reader gets the message exactly the way you want to convey and gets ready to put all-out efforts required to achieve the objective of the communication.
- You must be competent in the subject you are dealing with otherwise it may lack clarity both in terms of quality of

communication and the style of communication. Style of communication is a skill; you have to learn it by practice.

- Be confident when you are communicating verbally or in writing i.e. avoid using the words like "in my opinion", "I think", "probably" "… "Or similar", "… or equivalent", etc. as it reflects your confusion which worries the decision-maker as to whether he should go with your opinion or not.

- When you are confident, you will put your communication in a straight forward manner without mixing your emotions with the facts. This courage of yours will convince your reader that you have done your homework and it will result in immediate action in the matter, that's the main objective of effective business communication.

CHAPTER 06

Tenets of Public Procurement

"Honesty and transparency make you vulnerable. Be honest and transparent anyway"

– Mother Teresa

After the 2G scam was unearthed, there was a lot of hue and cry on corruption in public procurement. Therefore, to bring fairness and transparency to the public procurement system, the Government of India decided to introduce Public Procurement Law, and bill no. 58 of 2012 was passed by the cabinet. However, the bill could not be tabled in Parliament and therefore is not enacted as law to date. It is envisaged in the bill that:

The procuring entity shall, concerning public procurement, have the **responsibility** and **accountability** to:

a. Ensure efficiency, economy, and transparency;
b. Provide fair and equitable treatment to bidders;
c. Promote competition;
d. Ensure that the price of the successful bid is reasonable and consistent with the quality required;
e. Evolve mechanisms to prevent corrupt practices.

Before proceeding further let us get an understanding of these two words "responsibility" and "accountability".

These two words are derived from the Delegation of Powers which every executive is enjoying in the public sector depending on his level. Delegation of powers gives an executive "Authority" to take the decision. However, authority comes with the responsibility of ensuring correctness of the decision and in case the decision goes otherwise accountable for the decision taken by him.

I am delighted by the first tenet of the public procurement bill i.e to ensure "efficiency" because, in one word the importance of adherence to rules, procedure and guidelines have been clarified.

During deliberations on the subject, my favorite question to the participants is, what do you mean by efficiency here? Since I am dealing mainly with engineers, the most common reply is efficiency is output by input and we should give maximum output, etc. To make the things clear I then ask them to try and define the meaning of two words which we use very often i.e. Effectiveness and Efficiency. You have also used these words much time, do you want to try defining them. Please do! However, the simplest definition of these two words is:

> Effectiveness is "doing the right things", and
> Efficiency is "doing things right".

Thus, the meaning of 'efficiency' here is to do things rightly i.e. by following laid down rules, procedures, and guidelines. Further, it is the responsibility of the procuring official to ensure value for money and must also appear fair and transparent as has been discussed earlier.

Providing fair and equitable treatment to bidders:

I have found this tenet of public procurement as the biggest challenge in decision making and the root cause of delay in the decision-making process.

It is a fact that techno-commercial evaluation of the bids received is a time-consuming process in public procurement/job contracts. I have tried to analyze the reasons for such delays and dilemmas faced by the members of the techno-commercial evaluation committee (TEC) members.

Tenders in the public sector are generally issued by the concerned department where only one or two executives are entrusted with the job of finalizing special terms and conditions of the tender. My observations in this regard are as under:-

When it comes to mentioning experience for the particular job/area/project, it is mentioned in the tender that the bidder should have experience of executing a particular job or should have a "similar" experience. Now, it is a challenge for the TEC to find out whether the similar experience quoted by one of the bidders is similar or not.

The term which is quite often used in the tendered specifications for procurement is so and so size or "equivalent". Again, it is the responsibility of TEC to finally decide whether the specification quoted by the bidder is equivalent or not.

In many cases, you wish to procure items from preferred makes and mention your preference also in the tender. But the challenge comes, when someone quotes for an item, although not in your preferred list, which is matching all your specifications or maybe appearing even better than your specifications, whether to accept it or reject it and if you have to reject the quote, then on what grounds because "preference" is not a compulsion but a choice. Understand this with the following anecdote:

A high-level Indian delegation led by Prime Minister of India, Home Minister and other senior officials went to Russia for a high-level meeting convened between Russian Premier, Russian delegates, and Indian Delegation. Coffee was served during the meeting and after finishing their cup of coffee, many delegates kept the cup straight, few kept it upside down. Indian Home Minister finished his coffee and looked towards Prime Minister whose cup was still half-filled. As he was not sure how to place it, he kept it tilted on the saucer. Russian Protocol office was thoroughly confused, as they were aware of the meaning of the other two styles of cup keeping but not the tilted style. They checked the protocol books also but could not find the answer. Their Chief Protocol Officer rang his Indian counterpart to know the meaning. Indian officer was also not aware of the same but he asked Russian protocol officer to check it out from our Home Minister as he is a very humble and nice man and will not mind it. The Chief Protocol Officer of Russia mustered all the courage and went to Home Minister and politely asked him the meaning. The Home Minister slowly asked him, what is the meaning of keeping the cup straight? Sir, they want more coffee, and what is the meaning of keeping the cup facing down, Sir, they don't want more coffee. The Home Minister laughed slowly and said, you Russians are very nice people but very innocent, my style only tells, if you have more coffee, serve me, if you don't have, never mind.

I hope the meaning of preference is clear to you now. However, if you are very particular to go for specific brand, the more appropriate word "acceptable make" can be used which will be unambiguous and shall help you in accepting only what you want to 'accept'.

As regards promoting competition, CVC has time and again reiterated that the award of Government contracts through public auction/public tender is to ensure transparency in the public procurement, to maximize economy and efficiency in Government procurement, to promote healthy competition among the tenderers, to provide for fair and equitable treatment of all tenderers and to eliminate irregularities, interference and corrupt practices by the authorities concerned. This is required by Article 14 of the Constitution.

However, in rare and exceptional cases, for instance, during natural calamities and emergencies declared by the Government; where the procurement is possible from a single source only; where the supplier or contractor has exclusive rights in respect of the goods or services and no reasonable alternative or substitute exists; where the auction/tender was held on several dates but there were no bidders or the bids offered were too low, etc., this normal rule may be departed from and such contracts may be awarded through 'private negotiations'.

CVC vide circular dated 9th May 2006 has advised that while open tendering is the most preferred mode of tendering, even in the case of limited tendering, the Commission has been insisting upon transparency in the preparation of panel.

However, in many PSEs, we resort to single tendering as we have confidence in the vendor/contractor that he will provide the best material/services. That needs to be avoided as there is no scope for your perception in public procurement.

Further, we procure many items for years regularly from single vendor terming the same as 'Proprietary Item' as the same has to be procured from Original Equipment Manufacturer (OEM) only. It is to be noted that due diligence is required before making an item proprietary and it should resort to only when other technically acceptable substitutes are not available.

As regards reasonability of the L-1 (lowest rates) received, it is a challenging task for the decision-makers to certify that the price of the successful bid is reasonable and consistent with the quality required and therefore the file is sent to the agency who has prepared the 'estimate' to justify the reasonability of the L-1 rates. In most cases, negotiations with the party are recommended as they have no other means to justify the reasonability. Negotiations have been dealt with separately in the book.

As regards, evolving mechanisms to prevent corrupt practices, the systems/procedures and guidelines and also Delegation of Powers (DOP) issued from time to time are the efforts of management to ensure fairness and transparency in decision making at various levels.

CHAPTER
07

Enablers for Effective Decision Making

"Decision is the spark that ignites action. Until a decision is made, nothing happens... Decision is the courageous facing of issues, knowing that if they are not faced, problems will remain forever unanswered."

—Wilfred A. Peterson

After spending a good number of years in the vigilance department, it is my conviction that most of the executives in the Public Sector are fair, transparent, honest, sincere, and loyal to their organization, but they are very emotional i.e. so much emotionally attached to their duties and responsibilities that they knowingly or unknowingly deviate from the laid down procedure/guidelines to expedite the job in hand, to meet production targets, to raise performance levels, meet customers' demand, etc. which at times puts them into unwanted/unwarranted trouble.

It is a fact that decision-making in the public sector is guided by the rules, procedures, and guidelines. It is a general perception of most of the public sector executives that these procedures and guidelines are hindrances to their faster decision making.

Being associated with preparing many procedures and guidelines, I am convinced that these procedures and guidelines are their enablers in faster, logical, and effective decision making. I looked at the cartoon below on one of the websites and liked it very much as it facilitates in explaining the importance of rules and procedures in our professional lives.

I acknowledge my gratitude to the cartoonist who has prepared this cartoon which depicts the importance of rules, procedures, and guidelines in the public sector working.

It is a fact that the public sector executive is required to walk on the tight rope with a balancing rod (rules/procedures/guidelines) in his hand. Although he learns to walk on the tight rope over a while with his experience and can even run without taking the support of balancing rod except under the situation when he starts getting misbalanced i.e. when on cross-roads. Under such circumstances, these rules/procedures/guidelines come to his rescue to save him from falling. However, with his experience, maturity, and practice, an executive can take rational decisions without even referring to any rule/procedure/guideline in most cases.

It is only in approximately 10-15% cases when he finds himself at crossroads and he is confused i.e. misbalanced. Procedures/guidelines not only help him in taking the rational decision but also give him the confidence that his decision will not be challenged tomorrow even if anything goes wrong as he has followed the laid down procedure which has the requisite approval.

I strongly believe that while framing rules/procedures/guidelines, the objective is to protect organizational as well as employees' interests. Therefore, by adhering to the laid down rules, procedures, and guidelines, you are not only protecting the interests of the organization but also guaranteeing your safety and security.

To understand this, take the example of a "traffic signal". Are traffic signals on the road installed by the government are there to earn revenue for the government? Whether Traffic Policemen have been appointed for the sole purpose of levying fines for violation of the traffic rules and earning revenue for the Government?

The obvious answer will be "no". Traffic rules and signals are there to take care of our safety as well as the safety and security of other fellow commuters on the road. Government has no intention of levying fine to earn revenue otherwise they would have encouraged us to violate the rules to maximize revenue for the Government. Similarly, rules, procedures, and guidelines have been framed by your organization to help you in faster, correct, rational, and effective decision-making so also to protect you from frivolous complaints as you have seen above in the case of Ram and Shyam.

It reminds me of the incident which relates to the period when I was travelling frequently from Delhi to Ludhiana on weekends as my family was at Ludhiana and I was posted at Delhi. One evening, when I reached the bus stand, one Ajanta Roadways bus was ready to move and almost all the seats were already occupied. The driver of the bus called me inside and offered me a seat next to him. I thanked him for the nice gesture. The moment he took out the bus from the stand, he was in full mood and was speeding up. We were approaching the signal and it was Red though not crowded, he crossed the signal even when it was "RED". I asked him why he has not stopped the bus! He jokingly replied that we are KING on the road, why should we stop.

On the next signal, my heartbeat was going out of control as it was Red again but he cleanly crossed the bus on that signal too. Although frightened, I was sitting silent and praying to the almighty for my safety and the safety of my fellow passengers on the bus. On the next crossing, I took a sigh of relief as the signal was "Green" but to my utter surprise, the driver suddenly stopped the bus, I anxiously enquired from the driver, what happened? He coolly replied that I am not the only KING on the road, there are many others like me in my agency and are on the road.

Suppose, everybody starts making their own driving rules and follow them, will it be possible to drive? As rules of one may not be known to others and there will be every chance of collision. Thus, for the safety, security and well being of you as well as your Organization, such rules/procedures and guidelines are framed and updated/modified from time to time.

Systems and Procedures

Every organization develops certain systems to achieve its objective in a fair, efficient, and transparent manner. Systems are the mechanisms through which procedures are formulated, monitored, and controlled. It helps in:

- Building confidence
- Bringing transparency
- Reducing dependency
- Improving the decision-making process
- Building a foundation for improvement
- Bringing out discrepancies through the audit system

It must be kept in mind that every activity performed in an organization is a part of the system even if it appears to be a trivial one. Thus, it must be performed in a manner as stipulated. To understand this, please try and define the system. A 'word' you have heard and used many times. The simplest definition of a system is:

> **"System"** is a set of *procedures*,
> **"Procedure"** is a set of *processes*, &
> **"Process"** is a set of activities.

Thus, every activity performed in an organization is part of the system. In case, your decision is ever questioned, you can't absolve your responsibility by saying that this was a minor deviation from the laid down procedure or guidelines.

It reminds me of one more dilemma public sector executive face while taking a decision i.e. the difference between 'deviation' and 'violation' to the procedure. He is fully aware that violation of the procedure is misconduct but deviation i.e. minor here and there from the procedure must be allowed in the interest of the organization. That's his view but please remember, there is no minor or major deviation i.e. any deviation from the laid down procedure, if not approved by the Competent Authority, as per Delegation of Powers in your organization, shall be viewed as a violation of the procedure.

In one of the seminars, I heard our ex-CMD saying that we develop systems/procedures to manage the organization but over time these systems/procedures start managing us.

Thus, for all the delays in decision making, we start blaming systems/procedures. You ask any line manager for the quality of input material, the reply shall be that the quality is not good because we are bound to purchase from the lowest bidder as per the laid down procedure. This perception that we procure material/services only from the lowest bidder even compromising the quality of material/service is in the mind of most of the PSE executives.

Whereas this is a wrong perception and needs to be taken out from your minds immediately as we procure 'only' what we wish to procure. Therefore, we call bids generally in two parts i.e. "techno-commercial bid" and "price-bid". We open price bids of only those vendors/contractors who are found techno-commercially eligible i.e. they are ready to give what we want and on our terms and conditions. Then, where is the question of buying sub-standard items!

In the story of Ram & Shyam, the question itself was wrong! Because whether the action was right or wrong can be evaluated vis-à-vis some criteria i.e. laid down procedure/guideline and they were nowhere told in the story. Similarly, your actions/decisions will be evaluated vis-à-vis laid down procedure/guidelines of your Organization and if you have acted within the ambit of laid down procedures, you can never be held responsible, even if there is a loss to Organization. In that case, the investigating agency can only suggest 'System Improvement Measures' to plug the loophole.

CHAPTER 08

Negotiation – Commercial Issues

"Don't bargain yourself down before you get to the table."

— Carol Frohlinger

One of the biggest challenges in decision making in public procurement is "Negotiation" for envisaged procurement of material/services. The first question which strikes the mind is whether to negotiate as the lowest bidder has emerged out of the competition. Further, L-1 (lowest bidder) is aware that his rates are the lowest, why he will agree to negotiations. Even if negotiations are resorted to, what will be the basis for negotiation? Can we rely on the departmental estimate for negotiations?

During investigations, I have seen departmental estimates varying from the actual rates obtained in the range of +/- 100% or even more.

Let's try and find answers for these issues which keep hindering the decision making process. As already discussed in the previous chapter, the tenets of public procurement are as under:

The procuring entity shall, concerning public procurement, have the responsibility and accountability to:

a. Ensure efficiency, economy, and transparency;
b. Provide fair and equitable treatment to bidders;

c. Promote competition;

d. **Ensure that the price of the successful bid is reasonable and consistent with the quality required;**

e. Evolve mechanisms to prevent corrupt practices.

Thus, it's the responsibility of procuring officials to ensure that the lowest rates obtained out of the tendering process are reasonable!

Thus, it's a practice in many public sector enterprises that the recommending/approving authorities recommend negotiations in most of the procurement/contract cases to bring on records that the prices obtained are reasonable and they have been finalized after negotiations.

It appears to be a good practice but the challenge again is CVC guidelines on the subject. I wish to draw your attention to CVC Circular No. 4/3/07 dated 3rd March 2007 which stipulates that

"As post tender negotiations could often be a source of corruption, it is directed that there should be no post-tender negotiations with L1, except in certain exceptional situations."

CVC has further clarified that such exceptional situations would include, procurement of proprietary items, items with limited sources of supply, and items where there is suspicion of a cartel formation.

In cases where a decision is taken to go for re-tendering due to the unreasonableness of the quoted rates, negotiations would be permitted with L-1 bidder for the supply of bare minimum quantity, in case of emergencies.

The same CVC circular further stipulates that negotiation should not be allowed to be misused as a tool for bargaining with L-1 with dubious intentions or lead to delays in decision making.

Here comes the dilemma! CVC view negotiation as a "source of corruption" and we negotiate to ensure the reasonability of L-1 prices obtained.

In a Maharatna PSE, after receipt of the above referred circular, it was decided to modify the Purchase/Contract procedure of the company. The procedure was suitably modified to avoid negotiations stating as under:

"In case of open tenders, if four or more eligible bidders are available during the price-bid opening, the tender shall be finalized based on lowest rates obtained. However, in case it is felt that the rates are unreasonable, re-tendering shall be resorted to fairly and transparently.

In case of limited tender inquiries, if the lowest rates obtained are within the approved deviation range of departmental estimate, the tender shall be finalized on L-1 rates obtained. However, in the case of single tender cases, negotiations can be held with the approval of Competent Authority".

As per the procedure in vogue in that PSE, in case deviation to the laid-down procedure is required in exceptional circumstances, approval of Chief Executive shall be required and such deviations shall be reported to Vigilance Department also.

Believe me, within six months of implementation of this procedure, more than 25 deviation cases were reported to the vigilance department and in all the cases, approval of the Chief Executive was obtained for negotiation in the above-referred situations also where negotiation was banned.

It was, therefore, decided to modify the procedure suitably as it was resulting in a delay in decision making.

As mentioned above, it has become customary in most of the PSEs to negotiate with the lowest bidder to bring on records the reasonability of the lowest rates obtained and avoid further complications, if any, in this regard.

It's a fact that even the lowest prices obtained in PSEs are comparably higher than the market prices for the same product/services. The reason for the same has been dealt with in detail earlier in this book i.e. "Effort Cost".

Thus, we may conclude that negotiation is inevitable under such situations. However, negotiation is an art that has to be learned by practice.

Whereas, generally the negotiations being held in PSEs are done by the committee which consists of Technical, Finance, and Material Management officials, and none of them is trained in the art of negotiation.

Whereas, the team is required to negotiate with the vendors/suppliers/contractors that are into negotiation day in and day out and are a real expert in the art of negotiation.

I was also a member of many such committees and would like to share my experience. We generally call vendor/supplier to our office for negotiations on stipulated date and time. This job is handled by the Material Management Department (Purchase Department). Department after seeking approval of the Competent Authority for negotiation and for the officials who will be in the negotiating committee sends the letter to the party for attending negotiation meeting on stipulated date and time. Further, they inform the committee members also for negotiation with the party requesting them to be present on the stipulated date and time at a particular venue.

The vendor comes generally before the appointed time whereas the Material Management official has to call other committee members for the meeting. Although, they will come for the meeting but are they prepared for negotiations?

I have seen that many times, they will enquire from others about the issues to be discussed and the scope of reduction in the rates, etc. At the back of their mind, it's clear that this vendor who has been called for price negotiations has emerged as the lowest vendor in the competition, why he will further reduce his rates.

The negotiation starts with this perception in minds of the PSEs executives thus they start pleading with the vendor for some reduction in rates right from the beginning. Vendor being the seasoned player, he will express his inability to reduce the prices and even go to the extent and may say that in these rates, he will be suffering a loss but to maintain relations with the Company he is ready to supply the materials at the quoted rates. During discussions, he will give a clear hint that if desired, the company may go for re-tendering but the prices shall be higher in the next tender.

Do you think, any scope is left for the negotiating committee after all these deliberations? However, the committee will again plead for some reduction and he will reluctantly agree for half percent or one percent reduction in rates seeking many relaxations e.g. delivery period, timely payment of bills and/or settlement of earlier disputes, etc. It may also happen that this reduction also is obtained after two-three meetings, thus resulting in a delay in decision making.

During the Project review of a plant by the CVO of that PSE where the modernization and expansion program valuing several hundred crores was going on, it was observed that there was a delay of more than four months at the starting of one of the job. It was informed that the tender finalization was delayed due to protracted negotiations with the contractor. However, CVO noticed that the project cost was only Rs. 30 crores as it was a small job. CVO enquired about the L-1 rates and reduction obtained after negotiations. It was found that the L-1 bid was Rs 26.5 crores and the reduction obtained during negotiations was Rs. 30 lacs. As I was also attending the meeting with CVO, I had witnessed the furious reaction of CVO terming it as avoidable delay stating that more than this amount we could have saved if we would have started the project on envisaged time. Further, this delay will result in hampering the progress of other major on-going jobs.

From the above, it is clear that PSE executives are required to learn the art of negotiation including the executives from the technical stream also, as they are the end-users of the product/services and generally they raise indent along with an estimate for their requirements and therefore always part of such negotiation committees.

Let's discuss in brief the "art of negotiation" to the extent that it helps the decision-makers in taking effective and timely decisions when it comes to negotiations as negotiations are generally termed as time-consuming processes.

Although there are thousands of books available to teach you the art of negotiation and further there is "Google baba" to teach you anything you wish to learn. Here we will discuss the issues relating to negotiations in the PSE environment as discussed above. We have to negotiate to get the best rates possible and at the same time we have to appear fair and transparent in our approach. Isn't it a challenge!

From the scenario depicted above, you may feel, before the meeting starts, that you are in the 'weaker position'. However, this may be true for the other side also, but you will never know that until you go through the formal steps of negotiation. Therefore, assume that you have the upper hand and be confident from the outset or you will run the risk of getting "wiped out". You being on 'one side of the fence' have in your mind what you wish to achieve.

The question here is whether you have in your mind what you wish to achieve? Therefore the first attribute of a good negotiator is "KNOWLEDGE". The more knowledge you possess of the issues in question, the greater your participation in the process of negotiation. Please take it as a task assigned to you, the moment you get the information that you are on the committee for negotiation in a particular case. Try to gather knowledge about the product/service, rates at which you got the product earlier, current prevailing rates for the same/similar product/service, the difference between L-1 and L-2 rates, the reputation of the L-1 supplier, his order position, etc. Your little efforts in this direction shall give you confidence when you are at the negotiating table.

As negotiation is an art, it requires a lot of practice to be a good negotiator. You have to work on "SELF" i.e. your Self-confidence, Determination, Persistence, ability to manage stress, and ability to think out of the box. All these attributes shall be required during negotiation. Thus, you have to practice the skill to convert knowledge into action i.e. you have to be an effective communicator. Communication consists of 55% body language, 38% tone of voice, and only 7% spoken words. Therefore, you have to be very watchful about your posture, movement of hands, tone, etc. and also must learn to understand the body language of others as they may give you many signals through their body language during negotiations.

Furthermore, in the PSE environment, during price negotiations, you are required to discuss rates only, therefore, refrain from giving any relaxation on technical/commercial issues during negotiation. Please also keep in mind that during price negotiations, you are required to seek a reduction in prices and under no circumstances increase in rates should be accepted even when it comes to seeking a reduction in some items and accepting an increase in other items in case of multi-items/part/jobs tender although it may be resulting in overall reduction.

Negotiation in PSEs is seen as an extra burden as executives are already pre-occupied with other assigned responsibilities, they finish the negotiation and leave drafting minutes of the meeting on Purchase official. It is observed during investigation in several cases that what transpired during deliberations in the negotiation meeting is not found properly mentioned in the note resulting in a distorted perception of the whole negotiation process in the mind of investigating agencies.

It is, therefore, essential that the committee should sit together and draft the note mentioning the outcome of negotiations. Further, written communication must be taken from the vendor/supplier on the finally agreed rates before the award of the tender/contract to avoid any dispute at a later date.

CHAPTER 09

Scanning of Decisions in PSEs

"Even if a snake is not poisonous, it should pretend to be venomous"
— Chanakya

Record keeping in the public sector is a challenging task because we do not create these records for ourselves or our bosses but for the third parties who may not be aware of our style of working, our decision-making procedures, customs being followed in our organization, etc. However, they have the right and authority to look into our records and decide whether the right decision was taken and whether it was a logical, fair, and correct decision under the circumstances. As also indicated earlier, a public sector executive is also responsible to prove that the decision taken was the most appropriate decision under the situation in which it was taken. Further, he can be made accountable for the decision taken, if it is found wrong or inconsistent with the laid down procedures/guidelines.

Right from the day of his joining till the end of his career, Public Sector executive is always afraid of following three "C's" as he is aware that his decisions are always under the scanner of the following agencies:-

- Comptroller and Auditor General of India (CAG)
- Central Vigilance Commission (CVC)
- Central Bureau of Investigation (CBI)

Vigilance Functions

The point of interaction between Internal & External sources is primarily a Zone of Vigilance and interaction between various components of the Organization is Administrative.

To start with let us discuss vigilance functions as the name 'vigilance' is taken in PSEs with a negative connotation.

CVC has very nicely defined vigilance activities in its circular dated 13th April 2004 as under:

> *"The raison d'être of vigilance activity is not to reduce but to enhance the level of managerial efficiency and effectiveness in the organization."*

Commercial risk-taking forms part of the business. Therefore, every loss caused to the organization, either in pecuniary or non-pecuniary terms, need not necessarily become the subject matter of a vigilance inquiry. Thus, whether a person of common prudence, **working within the ambit of the prescribed rules, regulations, and instructions, would have decided in the prevailing circumstances in the commercial/operational interests of the organization is one possible criterion for determining the bona fides of the case.** A positive response to this question may indicate the existence of bona-fides. A negative reply, on the other hand, might indicate their absence.

As vigilance function is alien to most of the executives in the public sector, they are always under the impression that the vigilance department is always indulging in punitive activities. Whereas, the Vigilance department generally undertakes three types of activities:

- Preventive Vigilance
- Predictive Vigilance
- Punitive Vigilance

Preventive Vigilance

- To study and modify procedures, if required, to increase transparency and accountability
- To undertake a review of regulatory functions to avoid discretion in decision making
- To educate employees for creating awareness about rule provisions and simplifying the cumbersome procedures, if required.
- To identify gray areas that are prone to corruption and un-plug them. Also, suggesting ways for systemic improvement to avoid re-occurrence.
- To prepare a list of Officers of Doubtful Integrity (ODI) who are found to be lacking in integrity.
- To prepare the agreed list in consultation with CBI and also to ensure that the officers in ODI and Agreed List are not posted in sensitive posts.
- To ensure periodical rotation of employees
- To ensure preparation/modification/updating of Purchase/Contract and systems/procedures, etc.

Predictive Vigilance

- To undertake periodic inspections regularly.
- Conducting surprise checks of all units (including remote stations).
- Conducting CTE Type inspections.
- Investigating the observations in I/E report referred by CTEO.

Punitive Vigilance

- To verify all complaints received.
- Scrutiny of complaints from vigilance angle and undertaking investigation after checking veracity.

- To submit the vigilance investigation report to the Disciplinary Authority for Regular Departmental Action (RDA) under minor/major penalty.
- Vetting of charge sheet while ensuring that the charges are in-line with the Investigation Report.
- Monitoring appointment of Inquiry Officer (IO) and Presenting Officer (PO) in RDA cases and to ensure adherence to the stipulated schedule.
- Examination/Processing of Inquiry Officer's report.
- To check the timely issue of Penalty Order by Disciplinary Authority.
- Recommending any work for intensive examination by CTEO.

Punitive vigilance is one of the functions of the vigilance department. The only dilemma is *"vigilance functions on the preponderance of probability"* i.e. they generally investigate the case based on available documents/records and circumstances of the case (as they perceive) to prove the allegation or otherwise. Therefore, it becomes all the more necessary to keep the relevant documents/records generated during the time of taking a decision. For punitive vigilance activities, vigilance functions within the boundaries of vigilance angle as defined by CVC. Definition of vigilance angle as per CVC circular dated 13th April 2004 & 21st December 2005 is as under:-

"Vigilance angle is obvious in the following acts: -

- Demanding and/or accepting gratification other than legal remuneration in respect of an official act or for using his influence with any other official.
- Obtaining valuable things, without consideration, or with inadequate consideration from a person with whom he has or likely to have official dealings or his subordinates have official dealings or where he can exert influence.

- Obtaining for himself or for any other person any valuable thing or pecuniary advantage by corrupt or illegal means or by abusing his position as a public servant.
- Possession of assets disproportionate to his known sources of income.
- Cases of misappropriation, forgery or cheating, or other similar criminal offenses.

In most of the PSEs, executives are required to submit Annual Immovable Property Return (AIPR) every year. These returns are kept in records by Vigilance Department and handed over to CBI in case of complaints against the employees relating to possession of disproportionate assets as such complaints are investigated by CBI only. While filing AIPR, due care must be taken to place all the relevant facts on records.

a. There are, however, other irregularities where circumstances will have to be weighed carefully to take a view of whether the officer's integrity is in doubt. Gross or willful negligence; recklessness in decision making; blatant violations of systems and procedures; the exercise of discretion in excess, where no ostensible/public interest is evident; failure to keep the controlling authority/superiors informed in time – these are some of the irregularities where the disciplinary authority with the help of the CVO should carefully study the case and weigh the circumstances to conclude whether there is reasonable ground to doubt the integrity of the officer concerned.

b. Any undue/unjustified delay in the disposal of a case, perceived after considering all relevant factors, would reinforce a conclusion as to the presence of vigilance angle in a case".

It is often heard in PSU that "taking no decision is the best decision". However, it should be kept in mind that decision is required to be taken within a reasonable time as stipulated in procedures/guidelines of the PSE as any delay beyond the stipulated period shall be seen as misconduct on the part of the decision-maker, however, senior he/she may be.

Let us briefly discuss the role and functions of audit/investigating agencies.

Comptroller and Auditor General of India (CAG)

CAG is the supreme audit agency in India and is empowered to audit all expenses from the combined fund of the union or state governments.

Various audits are conducted in public sector undertakings by their internal audit departments, statutory audit, or CAG throughout the year to ensure compliance with rules, procedures, and guidelines.

Public Sector executives regularly deal with the Internal Audit department of their organization. Let us briefly discuss the Internal Audit functions.

Distinct from the statutory audits and Government Audits, internal audits are conducted at the behest of internal management to check the health of a company's finances and analyze an organization's operational efficiency. Internal audit is an independent function of management which entails the continuous and critical appraisal of the functioning as an entity, with a special focus on possible areas for improvement by strengthening and adding value to its governance mechanisms.

Internal auditors assist management with this task by providing a focus on risk management and the implementation of more stringent internal controls to manage prospective risks and vulnerabilities. Internal auditing teams enable management to direct efforts towards more risk-laden areas, thereby enhancing overall process efficiency and adding value to the existing set of resources. With IT's (Information Technology) increasingly critical role, the threat of data theft or loss due to system failure or hacking/espionage has become ever more acute. For addressing these new vulnerabilities, there is a heightened need for internal auditors able to identify and mitigate IT-associated risks.

With these factors in mind, there are many key advantages associated with internal audit.

1. The internal audit function, as an independent operation, is carried out objectively. This independence enables internal auditors to render an impartial and unbiased judgment essential to the proper conduct of business.
2. As a management function, internal audits are designed to serve management's needs via constructive recommendations in areas such as resource utilization and regulatory compliance.
3. Risk management through internal audit enables management to effectively mitigate risk and other associated uncertainties, thereby enhancing an organization's capacity to build value.

Internal audit in India has been made mandatory by the following provisions:

Section 177 of the Companies Act 2013 (Previously Section 292A of the Companies Act, 1956)

Section 177 of the Companies Act, 2013 requires the following to constitute an audit committee and require the internal auditor to attend and participate in the meetings of such audit committees:

1. Every listed company
2. Unlisted public companies with paid-up capital not less than INR 10 crores (US$ 166,666)
3. All private limited companies with paid-up share capital not less than INR 20 crores (US$ 333,333) or more
4. All companies with paid-up share capital below the threshold limit mentioned in (2) and (3) above, but with public borrowings from financial institutions, banks, or public deposits of rupees INR 50 crores (US$ 833,333) or more.

Keeping the importance of the internal audit function in mind, the Securities and Exchange Board of India (SEBI) introduced specific mandatory and recommendatory corporate governance provisions in Clause 49 of the Listing Agreement applicable to listed entities.

As per Clause 49, an audit committee is required to review the following:

1. Whether in the entity, the internal audit function is being made functional in proper order by reviewing the structure of the internal audit department, personnel recruited and seniority of the official who shall be heading the department, frequency of audits, and terms of remuneration of the chief internal auditor.
2. Internal audit reports relating to weaknesses found in internal controls.
3. The findings of any internal investigation by internal auditors into matters where there is suspected fraud or irregularity, or a failure of internal control systems of a significant impact.
4. The CEO and the CFO are required to certify to the Board of Directors that they accept responsibility for the effectiveness of internal controls and that they have disclosed to the auditors and the audit committee deficiencies in the operation of the internal controls if any, and steps have been taken for their rectification.

The above clauses and others are part of the Listing Agreement, with which every entity listed on Indian stock exchanges must comply.

It can additionally be concluded from the above that management as well as the audit committee needs extensive support from the internal audit department to provide a primary assurance about controls and compliances before giving the required reports/certificates or to appropriately review the aspects necessary to make informed decisions.

A question has been frequently asked by my participants during vigilance awareness sessions regarding the difference between AUDIT and VIGILANCE functions as both are ensuring strict compliance with rules/procedures/guidelines, etc. Yes, it is an interesting question as both the functions appear to be doing the same job. However, there is a major difference between the working of these departments.

The audit ensures strict compliance with rules/procedures/guidelines, etc. as mentioned above and in case any non-compliance is observed, they report the matter to concerned authorities for further necessary action. However, Vigilance doesn't stop after finding such irregularities or non-compliance with systems/procedures. They further investigate and find out as to who is responsible and based on their investigation recommend disciplinary action on such official(s) who are found guilty. This report of the Vigilance is called First Stage Advice (FSA). In case, Disciplinary Authority is convinced on the findings of Vigilance, he either recommends MINOR PENALTY if the charges are not serious or recommend inquiry into the matter in case of gross negligence, etc. and appoints Inquiring Authority.

After the inquiry, Inquiring Authority submits the report to Disciplinary Authority, who forwards the same to CVO for his Second Stage Advice (SSA) in the matter.

In case any irregularity/non-compliance/negligence are found in the case at least two persons have generally held responsible i.e. Initiating Authority and Approving Authority.

Central Vigilance Commission (CVC)

CVC is an apex Indian governmental body created in 1964 to address governmental corruption. It has the status of an autonomous body, free of control from any executive authority, charged with monitoring all vigilance activity under the Central Government of India, advising various authorities in central Government organizations in planning, executing, reviewing, and reforming their vigilance work.

All vigilance-related activities in Central public sector undertakings, being part of the Central Government are under the jurisdiction of CVC.

Functions

The CVC receives complaints about corruption or misuse of office and recommends appropriate action. Following institutions, bodies, or a person can approach CVC:

- Central Government
- Lokpal
- Whistle-Blowers

A whistleblower is a person, who could be an employee of a Company or a government agency, or outsider (e.g. media, higher government official or police) disclosing information to the public or some higher authority about any wrongdoing, which could be in the form of fraud, corruption, etc.

It is not an Investigating Agency. The CVC either gets the investigation done through the CBI or CVO in PSEs.

It is empowered to inquire into offenses alleged to have been committed under the Prevention of Corruption Act, 1988 by certain categories of public servants.

Its Annual Report gives the details of the work done by the Commission and points to systemic failures. Improvement and Preventive measures are also suggested in the report.

Vigilance Administration in Departments/Organizations is headed by the Chief Vigilance Officers (CVO) and the Commission's activities concerning inquiry or causing inquiry are supported by/carried out through the CVOs.

Complaints received in the Commission are scrutinized thoroughly and wherever specific and verifiable allegations of vigilance natures are noticed, the complaints are forwarded to the CVO/CBI to conduct inquiry/investigation into the matter and report to the Commission.

CVOs in all Departments/Organizations are appointed after prior consultation with the Commission.

Chief Technical Examiners' Organization (CTEO)

The Chief Technical Examiner's Organization constitutes the technical wing of the Commission and is manned by two engineers of the rank of Chief Engineer (designated as Chief Technical Examiners) with supporting engineering staff.

The main functions of CTEO are:

- Technical audit of construction works of Governmental organizations from a vigilance angle.
- Investigation of specific cases of complaints relating to construction works
- Assistance to CBI in their investigations involving technical matters and for evaluation of properties,
- Tendering of advice/assistance to the Commission and Chief Vigilance Officers in vigilance cases involving technical matters

Integrity Pact (IP)

To ensure transparency, equity, and competitiveness in public procurement, the Commission has been recommending the concept of Integrity Pact (IP) for adoption and implementation by the Government Organizations.

The Pre-bid Integrity Pact is a tool to help Governments, businesses, and civil society to fight corruption in public contracting. It binds both buyers and sellers to ethical conduct and transparency in all activities from pre-selection of bidders, bidding and contracting, implementation, completion, and operation related to the contract. This removes the insecurity of bidders, that while they may abjure bribery, but their competitors may resort to it and win the contract by unfair means.

Ministry of Finance, Department of Expenditure in the Manual for Procurement of Goods 2017 has mandated all government departments/undertakings to incorporate Integrity Pact depending on the nature of procurements/contracts above a threshold value. The nature of procurement and threshold of value is to be decided by the Ministries/Departments with approval of the Minister in charge. As guidance, the threshold should be such as to cover bulk (eighty to ninety percent by value) of its procurement expenditure.

The pact essentially envisages an agreement between the prospective vendors/bidders and the buyer, committing the persons/officials of both sides, not to resort to any corrupt practices in any aspect/stage of the contract. Only those vendors/bidders, who commit themselves to such a Pact with the buyer, would be considered competent to participate in the bidding process. In other words, entering into this Pact would be a preliminary qualification. The essential ingredients of the Pact include:

i. Promise on the part of the Procuring Entity to treat all bidders with equity and reason and not to seek or accept any benefit, which is not legally available;

ii. Promise on the part of bidders not to offer any benefit to the employees of the Procuring Entity not available legally and also not to commit any offense under Prevention of Corruption Act, 1988 or Indian Penal Code 1860;

iii. Promise on the part of bidders not to enter into any undisclosed agreement or understanding with other bidders concerning prices, specifications, certifications, subsidiary contracts; etc.

iv. Undertaking (as part of Fall Clause) by the bidders that they have not and will not sell the same material/equipment at prices lower than the bid price;

v. Foreign bidders to disclose the name and address of agents and representatives in India and Indian Bidders to disclose their foreign principals or associates;

vi. Bidders to disclose the payments to be made by them to agents/brokers or any other intermediary;

vii. Bidders to disclose any past transgressions committed over the specified period with any other company in India or Abroad that may impinge on the anti-corruption principle;

viii. Integrity Pact lays down the punitive actions for any violation.

ix. Integrity Pact (IP) would be implemented through a panel of Independent External Monitors (IEMs):

IEMs shall be appointed by the organization in consultation with Central Vigilance Commission. Names and contact details of the Independent External Monitor(s) should be listed in Notice Inviting Tender (NIT). The IEM would review independently and objectively, whether and to what extent parties have complied with their obligations under the Pact. Government of India organizations and Public Sector Undertakings desirous of implementing Integrity Pact are required to select at most three persons (below the age of 70 (seventy) years) of high integrity and reputation as Independent External Monitors (IEM) after due diligence and forward to the CVC for its approval. Only those officers of Government of India Departments or Public Sector Undertakings, who have retired from top management positions, would be considered for appointment as IEM, provided they are neither serving nor retired from the same organization. Eminent persons retired judges of High/Supreme Courts, executives of the private sector of considerable eminence could also be considered for functioning as Independent External Monitors. The appointment of Independent External Monitors would be for an initial period of three years and could be extended for another term of two years (maximum tenure of five years).

Names and contact details of the Independent External Monitor(s) should be listed in Notice Inviting Tender (NIT).

x. In tenders meeting the criteria of threshold value/nature of procurement: Integrity Pact clause and format should be included in the Bid Documents. Each page of such an Integrity pact Performa would be duly signed by Purchaser's competent signatory. All pages of the Integrity Pact are to be returned by the bidder (along with the technical bid) duly signed by the same signatory who signed the bid, i.e. who is duly authorized to sign the bid and to make binding commitments on behalf of his company. Any bid not accompanied by Integrity Pact duly signed by the bidder shall be considered to be a non-responsive bid and shall be rejected straightway.

xi. Role/Functions of IEMs: The Monitors would not be subject to instructions by the representatives of the parties and should perform their functions neutrally and independently. They would review independently and objectively, whether and to what extent parties have complied with their obligations under the Integrity Pact.

For this purpose, they would have access to all contract documents/books of accounts of the bidders in case of any allegation of violation of any provisions of the Integrity Pact or payment of a commission, whenever required. The IEMs will have the option to participate in such meetings among the parties related to the project provided such meetings could have an impact on the contractual relations between the parties. Ideally, all IEMs of an organization should meet once every two months to take stock of the ongoing tendering process. The IEMs would examine all complaints received by them and give their recommendations/views to the designated officer of the Procuring Entity, at the earliest. The Monitors would also inform the Procuring Entity if they notice or have reason to believe, a violation of the Integrity Pact. They may also send their report directly to the Central Vigilance Commission, in case of suspicion of serious irregularities requiring legal/administrative action. At least one IEM would be invariably cited in the NIT.

However, for ensuring the desired transparency and objectivity in dealing with the complaints arising out of any tendering process, the matter should be examined by the full panel of IEMs, who would look into the records, conduct an investigation, and submit their joint recommendations. The recommendations of IEMs would be like advice and would not be legally binding. IEMs may not be equated with consultants in the Procuring Entity. Their role is independent and the advice once tendered would not be subject to review.

The role of the Chief Vigilance Officer (CVO) of the Procuring Entity shall remain unaffected by the presence of IEMs. A matter being examined by the IEMs can be separately investigated by the CVO if a complaint is received by him or directed to him by the CVC.

CVC's Jurisdiction

- Members of All India Service serving in connection with the affairs of the Union and Group A officers of the Central Government
- Officers of the rank of Scale V and above in the Public Sector Banks
- Officers in Grade D and above in Reserve Bank of India, NABARD, and SIDBI
- Chief Executives and Executives on the Board and other officers of E-8 and above in Schedule 'A' and 'B' PSEs
- Chief Executives and Executives on the Board and other officers of E-7 and above in Schedule 'C' and 'D' PSEs
- Managers and above in General Insurance Companies
- Senior Divisional Managers and above in LIC etc.

Central Bureau of Investigation (CBI)

CBI is the premier investigative agency of India. The CBI is overseen by the Ministry of Personnel, Public Grievances, and Pensions of the Federal government, headed by a Cabinet Minister who reports directly to the Prime Minister. The CBI, being a Union subject, may investigate:

- Offenses against central-government employees, or concerning affairs of the central government and employees of central public-sector undertakings and public-sector banks

- Cases involving the financial interests of the central government
- Breaches of central laws enforceable by the Government of India
- Major fraud or embezzlement; multi-state organized crime
- Multi-agency or international cases.

Over the years, CBI has built up an image for professionalism and integrity. The services of its investigating officers are sought for all major investigations in the country. CBI as an organization is held in high esteem by the Supreme Court, the High Courts, the Parliament, and the public. It is also involved in the collection of criminal intelligence on three of its main areas of operation, i.e.

- Anti-Corruption
- Economic Crimes, and
- Special crimes.

The Anti-Corruption Division of the CBI has handled cases against politicians, bureaucrats, CMDs of Banks, Financial Institutions, Public Sector Undertakings, etc. The following broad categories of criminal cases are handled by the CBI:

Cases of corruption and fraud committed by public servants of all Central Govt. Departments, Central Public Sector Undertakings, and Central Financial Institutions. Economic crimes, including bank frauds, financial frauds, Import-Export & Foreign Exchange violations, large-scale smuggling of narcotics, antiques, cultural property and smuggling of other contraband items, etc

As may be seen from the above, these agencies have clearly defined roles, thus, there is no need to be afraid of these agencies by any honest executive. However, I must admit that the fear of these agencies helps public sector executives in taking a fair, transparent, logical, and rational decision.

CHAPTER 10

Decision-Making Process

"When you have collected all the facts and fears and made your decision, turn off all your fears and go ahead."

— George S. Patton

Before we deliberate on the decision-making process, let's quickly go through the characteristics of decision making:-

- Decision making implies choices
- Continuous activity/process
- Mental/intellectual activity
- Based on reliable information/feedback
- Goal-oriented process
- Means and not the end
- Relates to a specific problem
- Time-consuming activity
- Needs effective communication
- Pervasive process
- Responsible job

Keeping in view the above characteristics of decision making, decision-maker may follow the under mentioned decision-making process to arrive at the most effective decision:

- Define The Problem
- Identify the Limiting Factors
- Develop Potential Alternatives
- Analyze the Alternatives
- Select the Best Alternatives
- Implement the Decision
- Establish a Control and Evaluation System

(i) Define the Problem

The most important part of the decision-making process is to define the problem. However, in day-to-day professional lives, most of the decision-makers are so busy that they try to spend minimum time understanding the real problem and make a decision on the issue which is visible to them although that may not be the root cause of the problem. Let's understand it with an example.

We have a beautiful circular lawn in front of our office well illuminated with eleven poles having decorated lamps. While leaving office, our Chief Executive observed that bulb on one of the pole was not working he called Maintenance Manager and advised him to get it changed. The maintenance Manager told the electrician to change the bulb and went home. After a few days, CE again noticed that the bulb on the same pole was not working he called Maintenance Manager and fired him for his negligence. Maintenance Manager scolded electrician for not obeying his instructions though electrician told that he had changed the bulb. However, the Maintenance Manager asked him to change the bulb in his presence. Incidentally, after a few days, Chief Executive again observed that the bulb on the same pole is fused. This time he went out of control and charged the Maintenance Manager and his team for gross negligence in maintenance work. As the bulb was replaced last time in his presence, the Maintenance Manager could not digest this firing and decided to check the underground cable the next day morning. Accordingly, workers were arranged, and digging was done and cable was checked. It was found that the cable was having a problem and the bulb was getting damaged due to cable fault. The cable was repaired and the same bulb is still working.

(ii) Identify Limiting Factors

We have to take a decision keeping in mind the resources i.e. what all is available to us e.g. money, manpower, material, time, etc. and so also our constraints i.e. what may not be available to us even if it may be of great help to us. For example, one of the machines in your mill is giving you trouble for quite some time resulting in more downtime for its maintenance. You decided to replace it with the new machine and initiated a proposal for procuring a new machine but your proposal is turned down by finance stating budget constraints. Thus, the decision taken by you to replace the machine resulted only in a waste of time as you have to now think of other alternatives.

(iii) Develop Potential Alternatives

You are deciding because you have a problem to solve. It may so happen that you will immediately get an idea to get rid of your problem. Don't try to jump on the solution which has come to your mind as there may be many other alternatives to resolve the issue. Identify each such alternative that can help you in solving the issue. At times, out of box thinking may give you a better solution.

(iv) Analyze the Alternatives

Now, you have many ways to solve your problem. Analyze them vis-à-vis resources required for adopting a particular alternative and constraints you may face. As discussed earlier, constraints may be finances, manpower, a paucity of time, other pressures, etc.

(v) Select the Best Alternative

Out of the alternative analyzed as above, you may be able to select the alternative which is meeting all your requirements of budget, time, manpower, etc. and is most appropriate under the given situation/ circumstances. Select the alternative i.e. decide to implement the best alternative.

(vi) Implement the Decision

When we were talking of characteristics of decision making, we observed that one of the characteristics of decision making i.e. "decision making is mean and not the end". Please keep in mind that making a decision is only a means to resolve the issue but the problem can be solved only when the decision taken is implemented.

(vii) Establish a Control and Evaluation System

Always keep in mind that you have implemented a decision selecting the best possible alternative to get the envisaged results. Therefore, it is utmost necessary to establish a control and evaluation system to monitor its outcome.

CHAPTER 11

Philosophy of Decision Making

"Integrity without knowledge is weak and useless, and knowledge without integrity is dangerous and dreadful."

– Samuel Johnson

You are now well equipped to take effective decisions in a public sector scenario i.e. you have to ensure that your decision is fair, transparent, logical, rational, and within the boundaries of rules, procedures, and guidelines prevailing in your organization on the day of the decision. However, there is a philosophy behind decision making which shall also influence your decision making, let's briefly discuss the same before we proceed to decision making in the following cases:

We have talked of values at the beginning. Let's briefly discuss what are values? Our values determine what is right and what is wrong, and doing what is right or wrong is what we mean by ethics. To behave ethically is to behave in a manner consistent with what is right or moral. Philosophers have deliberated on the following philosophies of decision making and believe me while deciding on any scenario, these philosophies influence our decision.

The Utilitarian Approach

Utilitarianism was conceived in the 19th century by Jeremy Bentham and John Stuart Mill. They suggested that ethical actions are those that provide the greatest balance of good over evil.

- To analyze an issue using the utilitarian approach:
- Identify the various courses of action available
- Ask who will be affected by each action and what benefits or harms will be derived from each.
- Choose the action that will produce the greatest benefits and the least harm.

The ethical action is the one that provides the greatest good for the greatest number.

The Rights Approach

The second important approach to ethics has its roots in the philosophy of the 18th-century thinker Immanuel Kant and others like him. They focused on the individual's right to choose for him:

- People have dignity based on their ability to choose freely what they will do with their lives.
- They have a fundamental moral right to have these choices respected.
- People are not objects to be manipulated;
- It is a violation of human dignity to use people in ways they do not freely choose.

Many different, but related, rights exist besides this basic one. These other rights can be thought of as different aspects of the basic right to be treated as we choose:

- The right to the truth
- The right to privacy
- The right not to be injured
- The right to what is agreed, etc.
- As per the Rights Approach, we must ask,
- Does the action respect the moral rights of everyone?

Actions are wrong to the extent that they violate the rights of individuals.

The Fairness or Justice Approach

This approach is based on the teachings of the ancient Greek philosopher Aristotle, who said that:

> "Equals should be treated equally and un-equals unequally."

The basic moral question in this approach is: How fair is an action? Does it treat everyone in the same way, or does it shows favoritism and discrimination? Both favoritism and discrimination are unjust and wrong.

The Common-Good Approach

This approach to ethics assumes a society comprising individuals whose own good is inextricably linked to the good of the community. Community members are bound by the pursuit of common values and goals.

In this approach, the focus is on ensuring that the social policies, social system, institutions, and environment on which we depend are beneficial to all e.g. affordable health care, effective public safety, peace among nations, a just legal system, and an unpolluted environment. Appeals to the common good urge us to view ourselves as members of the same community.

The Virtue Approach

The virtue approach to ethics assumes that there are certain ideals toward which we should strive, which provide for the full development of our humanity. These ideals are discovered through thoughtful reflection on what kind of people we have the potential to become.

Virtues are attitudes or character traits that enable us to be and to act in ways that develop our highest potential. Honesty, courage, compassion, generosity, fidelity, integrity, fairness, self-control, and prudence are all examples of virtues. Virtues are like habits once acquired, they become characteristic of a person.

A person who has developed virtues will be naturally disposed to act in ways consistent with moral principles. A virtuous person is an ethical person. The focus of this approach is on what kind of person should I be? What will promote the development of character within me and my community?

Ethical Problem Solving

These five approaches suggest that once facts are ascertained, we should ask ourselves five questions when trying to resolve a moral issue:

- What benefits and what harms will each course of action produce, and which alternative will lead to the best overall consequences?
- What moral rights do the affected parties have, and which course of action best respects those rights?
- Which course of action treats everyone the same, except where there is a morally justifiable reason not to and does not show favoritism or discrimination?
- Which course of action advances the common good?
- Which course of action develops moral virtues?

While attempting to make an ethical decision, you have to develop potential alternatives and then look for answers to the above questions. It may also happen that only one of these approaches may be found most suitable under the given situation. Your challenge will be to find the one and then take the appropriate decision.

Let's look into certain situations and try taking decisions that may fit into one of the above-mentioned approaches.

Exercise on Ethical Problem Solving

"Ethics is knowing the difference between what you have a right to do and what is right to do."

– Potter Stewart

Please read each of the situations below and see if you can reach a solution meeting the criteria suggested by the three different approaches (Utilitarian, Justice, and Moral Rights):

1. Based on an evaluation of Skill, Knowledge, and Aptitude (SKA), your company has determined that two jobs (job A and job B) are equal. However, when you studied the labor market, you found out that applicant for job A are plentiful whereas those for job B are very limited. Should you offer less to those who apply for job A or should the pay be equal?

   "Equals should be treated equally and un-equals unequally."

2. Assume that the supply of electrical technicians is low so a firm hires a group of them at Rs. 18 per hour. Two years later, due to a recession, the supply of technicians is high so the market rate for them is now Rs. 15 per hour. Should the firm pay new hires Rs. 18 or Rs. 15? Given that the firm bases pay on supply

and demand, should it lower the pay of existing electricians to Rs. 15?

"Actions are wrong to the extent that they violate the rights of individuals"

3. Mr. Sharma is given an extremely large raise because of his superb work record for one year. As a result, he is currently earning Rs. 75,000 whereas others at the firm holding the same job are earning Rs. 45,000. Management expects Sharma to continue to excel and enhance the entire unit's productivity. Unfortunately, Sharma's performance drops off after the first year and his performance is now just average. What should be done about his pay? Should it be reduced to reflect his current performance or should he continue to earn more than all of the others?

"Both favoritism and discrimination are unjust and wrong."

4. Next year, Mr. Gupta's performance is truly spectacular, just as good as Sharma's had been in the previous case. Moreover, let's further assume that the company has no raise money available that year so no one, including Gupta, receives a merit raise. Given that Sharma received a large raise for past performance, is this fair to Gupta?

"The ethical action is the one that provides the greatest good for the greatest number."

5. Radha and Meera both work in the same department. Radha believes that Meera is being paid considerably more than she is. Both employees are being paid about the same amount. Radha complains to her boss and the HR manager and wants a pay raise. What should the HR manager say, assuming the firm follows the policy of not revealing the pay of individual employees? Should Radha be told the amount of Meera's pay? Or, should Radha only be told that there is a "misunderstanding' and that her belief is incorrect? Or, should some other approach be taken?

"Does the action respect the moral rights of everyone?"

6. When Radhika was hired she was told verbally that she would receive a raise when she finished her college degree and yet another raise when she was given added responsibility. She accepted the job offer based on this understanding. However, during the next two years, the firm experienced slow sales and has asked all factory employees to accept a 12% pay decrease. But, Radhika, who does not work in the factory, has finished college and has accepted more responsibility. Should she receive a raise?

"Actions are wrong to the extent that they violate the rights of individuals"

7. Two firms in the chemical solvent industry decide to merge. Employees in the testing department of firm A have enjoyed high pay for many years. However, firm A is purchased by firm B who has a history of paying low wages. As a result, employees in firms A's testing department earns on average Rs. 10.00 more per hour than those at firm B. Upon completion of the merger, what wage levels should prevail? Should wages be cut for those who worked for firm A? Or, should wages be increased for those in firm B?

"The ethical action is the one that provides the greatest good for the greatest number."

8. Ms. Sangeeta is a fifty-five-year-old employee of company A. Her children are out of college and her parents have both died. Company "A" offers a child care program to all employees along with an elder care program. However, Sangeeta, like many other employees, does not need these services, neither now or in the future. Should the firm retain these programs? Should alternative benefits for employees who have no use for such services be offered?

"Equals should be treated equally and un-equals unequally."

9. Daisy works as an accountant for a firm in the textile industry. During non-working hours she does extensive volunteer work for the Indian Red Cross, Meals on Wheels, and the National Heart

Association. Daisy's employer wants to maintain a favorable image in the community so it wants every employee to donate money to the Indian Red Cross. Should the firm pressure Daisy donate money? Keep in mind that if Daisy doesn't donate money, other employees may not either which could result in the firm having an unfavorable image in the community. On the other hand, Daisy already donates time which has a monetary value and she may feel that it is unfair to be asked to donate even more.

"Actions are wrong to the extent that they violate the rights of individuals"

10. Nandan works 25 hours per week for a mail-order firm in the packaging department. He receives no benefits other than those required by law. Nandan does the same work as three other employees all of whom work full time. These employees qualify for pensions, medical care, long term disability, child care, etc. Is this ethical? Assume that Nandan would like to work full-time, really wants to receive benefits, and feels harmed because of his shortfall. On the other hand, the firm is not legally required to pay Nandan benefits, Nandan only works part-time, and it would be expensive to pay benefits to all part-time employees, including Nandan.

"Equals should be treated equally and un-equals unequally."

CHAPTER 12

Factors Influencing Decision Making

"Whatever course you decide upon, there is always someone to tell you that you are wrong. There are always difficulties arising which tempt you to believe that your critics are right. To map out a course of action and follow it to an end requires courage."

– Ralph Waldo Emerson

Public sector executives are always required to make rational decisions and as you know, rationality relies mostly on logic and quantitative analysis. You consciously analyze possible alternative(s), formulate the main criteria for judging the expected outcomes of various alternatives, and assign weights to those alternatives to reflect their relative importance. Then, based on the expected outcomes and their weights, you rate your options by their perceived utility and choose the alternative that has the highest rating.

However, as the expected outcome involves uncertainty, in your ratings, you will need to incorporate the perceived risks in different possibilities. Thus, the first factor influencing your decision making is 'perception'.

Perception

What is Perception?

In simple words, perception can be defined as the act of seeing what is there to be seen. But what is seen is influenced by the:

 i. The Perceiver
 ii. The object
 iii. The situation

i. The Perceiver

The perceiver, the individual perceiving the decision, will be heavily influenced by his characteristics. The types of personal characteristics that can affect an individual's perception include:

- His background and experience
- Personal Values
- Personal Expectations
- Personal Interests

The decision making is influenced by the following factors when it comes to perceiver:

- Mood (optimism, pessimism)
- Rationality. Logic prevails (at all costs)
- Priorities
- Pressure
- Perceived risks
- Real Risks
- Personal stake

- Expectations
- Perspective, etc. etc...

ii. The Object

The object, which refers to any person, item, or event which can have an impact on the way it is perceived (Not clear). The relation an object has to other objects can also affect the perception of the perceiver. Let us try and understand it with an example:

Suppose you are Head of the Department of a Rolling Mill where one motor is installed by M/s. SIEMENS around 10 years back is now due for replacement. In the last ten years, this motor has given you trouble-free service and you are very much satisfied with its performance. You initiated a note for replacement of this motor with a motor of the same brand i.e. SIEMENS. However, when you went to your Mill In-charge, he suggested to include other reputed brands also to avoid single tender purchase e.g. Kirloskar, Cummins, etc. and go for procurement on Limited Tender Enquiry (LTE) basis to invite the competition. You found his logic correct and modified your proposal for procurement on an LTE basis within a few reputed known parties. However, when the proposal was sent for final approval of Chief Executive, he called you and handed over the brochure of a reputed manufacturer who is manufacturing the same type of motor and suggested looking into it saying that the representative of this manufacturer called on him a few days back. You looked into the brochure and found it technically suiting your requirement, you decided to go for calling quotes on open tender enquiry basis thinking that few more manufacturers may have come to the market in last ten years manufacturing the same type of motor and they should also get an opportunity to quote on the one hand and the other hand, you will also get the most competitive quotes.

Here, the object in question was the same i.e. motor, but the perception of three individuals was different for the same object.

iii. The Situation

Time, location, and other situational factors can influence our perception of an object.

It is a fact that every decision is taken considering the situation i.e. urgency, emergency, criticality, IR issues, etc. etc. but all such environmental issues are related to the perception of the perceiver. During my tenure in the vigilance department, I witnessed such situations several times when the concerned executive was trying to defend his decision explaining the situation under which he was compelled to take that decision e.g. his production could have stopped, delay in the decision could have resulted into IR issues, time pressure, other related environmental issues, etc. whereas in the opinion of vigilance no such urgency/emergency was visible from records shown to vigilance.

It reminds me of one more dilemma being faced by the public sector executives while making decisions i.e. to differentiate between "urgency" and "emergency". At times the urgent situation is also perceived as an emergency and procedures are circumvented in the name of emergency. I have asked this question to my participants many times, can you tell me the difference between these two words i.e. urgency and emergency?

Before proceeding further, may I request you to take a pause and think of the answer; I have got many answers to this question but the best one was "extreme urgency is emergency". Generally, emergencies are situations that can't be foreseen. Therefore, in many public sectors, very liberal procedures are framed to mitigate emergencies. However, there is no relaxation given in the procedures/guidelines of PSUs to mitigate urgencies for the simple reason that urgencies are man-made i.e. delay the decision, the day will come when it will become urgent and delay it further, it may lead to disaster thus resulting in an emergency. However, such emergencies are seen by the investigating agencies as "Created Emergencies", thus not absolving the decision-maker from his responsibilities/accountability. This has been explained in detail in a case-let given in the book.

Intuitive Decision-Making Process

In such situations, intuition can make you a much more effective decision-maker, especially when you are dealing with non-standard situations or in need of expeditious decision making. Let's briefly discuss the intuitive decision-making process. However, before dealing with the intuitive decision-making process, let's be clear in our mind that the decision you are taking is for mitigating official exigency/emergency and you are going to spend public money. Therefore, keep in mind that your intentions should be visible in such type of decision making also. Take my words, intentions do matter, and investigating agencies do care for your intentions also while investigating a matter.

Under the following situations/circumstances, an intuitive decision-making approach can help the decision-maker in effective decision making:-

- Where expedient decision making and rapid response is required. The circumstances leave you no time to go through the complete rational analysis.
- The factors on which you base your analysis change rapidly.
- The problem is poorly structured.
- The factors and rules that you need to take into account are hard to articulate unambiguously.
- You have to deal with ambiguous, incomplete, or conflicting information.
- Last but not the least, there is no precedent.

Let's discuss the meaning of intuition in the context of decision making. While there are many definitions of this aspect of decision making, there are three key features that characterize the intuitive mode of thinking:

The process is dominated by the subconscious mind, even if we use our conscious mind to formulate or rationalize the final results. The information is processed in parallel rather than sequentially i.e. instead of going through a logical sequence of thoughts one by one, we see the situation more as a whole, with different fragments emerging in parallel. We are more connected with our emotions e.g. it may occur in our mind that an option we consider does not feel right, even though there is no clear logic to prove that.

The first important thing to keep in mind is that even when we rely on intuition, it is still very important to do homework. The intuition will help us navigate faster through much of unstructured data and can work around certain gaps and conflicts in the available information. Yet, even intuition can be misled if too many of our facts are wrong or missing.

Another important thing is to pay attention to our emotional state while making an intuitive decision for if we are stressed or in a bad mood, the inner voice will be distorted or lost in the background of our strong feelings. A similar effect may happen with strong positive feelings. If we have to hear our inner voice, we have to get over our strong feelings.

Finally, the quality of intuitive decisions can be greatly increased if we include certain elements of the analytical approach i.e. try to follow the procedure of rational analysis first, as much as possible. Capture on paper the ideas on the main options and the criteria for evaluating the choices. We need to write down the key facts and factors which we should keep in mind.

This procedure is an effective way to feed our subconscious mind with all the relevant data it needs. It will help even more if we put all those notes together on paper as a mind map. It will help us if we keep all the important points written in one place and it shall also unclutter our mind. At that stage, we are much more ready to listen to our inner voice.

Organizational Issues

Decision making in the Public Sector has to be within the organizational boundaries, therefore, all your decisions shall be affected by many organizational issues, such as:

- Organizational Policies, Procedures & Guidelines
- Organizational Hierarchy
- Organizational Behavior

A. Organizational Policies, Procedures & Guidelines

As discussed earlier also, in the public sector we are not only bound to make logical and rational decisions but the greatest challenge is to appear taking the rational decision. To prove logic behind every decision taken may be a difficult task so long we are not adhering to laid down procedures and guidelines while taking a decision. Therefore, we have to always keep in mind the boundaries within which decisions can be taken in an organizational context and we must respect laid-down procedures and guidelines relating to the area in which we are required to make a decision.

B. Organizational Hierarchy

Most of the Public Sector Organizations have a vertical hierarchy set up in their Organizations i.e. starting from Chief Executive to down below level. Every executive in the organization is bestowed with some powers which we commonly know by the name of Delegation of Powers. These Delegations must be strictly adhered to while making a decision.

Delegation of Powers

Delegation of Powers is a division of Authority and powers downwards to the Subordinates to achieve the Organizational Objective i.e. sub-division and allocation of powers to subordinates for empowering them to achieve desired results by effective utilization of given powers.

Elements of Delegation

i. Authority

Authority is the power and right given to a person to use and allocate the resources efficiently, to take decisions, and to give orders to achieve the

Organizational Objectives. It always flows from top to bottom. It may, however, be noted that delegating the authority to someone else doesn't mean escaping from accountability. Accountability still rests with the person having the utmost authority.

ii. Responsibility

It is the responsibility of the official to whom power is delegated to ensure that the task assigned is completed as per laid down rules/procedures/guidelines. The person responsible for a job is answerable either way i.e. whether the job is completed or not completed. However, responsibility flows from bottom to top. Therefore, responsibility without adequate authority leads to discontentment and may become a hindrance to decision making.

iii. Accountability

As power always comes with responsibility, the authority empowered by the Delegation of Powers is answerable for variance in actual performance vis-a-vis target. It may be noted that powers cannot be sub-delegated by the authority to which it is given, thus accountability for a decision taken cannot be escaped by the official to whom powers have been delegated.

C. Organizational Behavior

Employees naturally behave differently at work than they do in social settings, largely due to the structured organizational environment of business. A variety of factors influence organizational behavior, including the company's structure, policies, and procedures, management effectiveness, and interactions between colleagues. All of these elements can inspire employees to work harder or contribute to their disengagement.

Power, authority, and politics all operate inter-dependently in the workplace. Understanding the appropriate ways, as agreed upon by the workplace rules and general ethical guidelines, in which these elements are exhibited and used are key components to running a cohesive business.

An excellent employment relationship is based on trust in the organization. Trust between employees and managers delivers positive outcomes in an organization. Trust between workgroup members helps members identify themselves with their workgroups. Organizations need to build trust among their employees for their well-being at work.

Participation in decision-making processes gives employees a sense of belongingness toward the organization by considering their opinion on important matters. To reciprocate such privileged actions, employees would exhibit identification and loyalty with their organization. Employees who participate in decision making may be motivated to deliver better performance because they feel very happy when their opinions are considered while making decisions.

Environment

Decision making is also influenced by environmental issues that are the external and internal factors that affect the organization. Simply, factors outside the organization are the elements of the external environment. The organization has no control over how the external environment will shape up. The external environment can be subdivided into 2 layers:

- Task Environment,
- General Environment

I. Task Environment of Organization

The task environment consists of factors that directly affect and are affected by the organization's operations. These factors include:

a. Competitors

Policies of the organization are often influenced by their competitors. In a competitive marketplace, companies are always trying to stay and go further ahead of their competitors. In the present business scenario, the competition and competitors in all respects have increased tremendously. The positive effect of this competition is that the customers always have options thus the overall quality of products goes high.

b. Customers

In today's business, "Satisfaction of Customers" is the primary goal of every organization. It is the customer who pays money for the organization's product or services. Decision-makers must pay close attention to customers' dimensions of the task environment because it's the customer purchase that keeps a company alive.

c. Suppliers

Suppliers are the providers of production or service materials. Dealing with suppliers is an important task of management. A good relationship between the organization and the supplier is important to keep a steady flow of quality input material/services.

d. Regulators

Regulators are units in the task environment that have the authority to control, regulate, or influence an organization's policies and practices. Government agencies are the main player of the environment and interest groups are created by its members in an attempt to influence the organization as well as the government. Trade Unions and the Chamber of Commerce are the common examples of an interest group.

e. Strategic Partners

Strategic Partners are the organization and/or the individuals with whom the organization enters into an agreement or understanding for the benefit of the organization. These strategic partners in some way influence the organization's activities in various ways.

II. General Environment of Organization

The general environment consists of factors that may not have an immediate direct effect on operations but influence the activities of the organization. The dimensions of the general environment are broad and non-specific. The elements of the general environment include:

a. Economic Dimension

The economic dimension is the overall status of the economic system under which the organization operates. The important economic factors for business are inflation, interest rates, and unemployment.

b. Technological Dimension

The technological dimension denotes the methods available for converting resources into products or services. Managers must be careful about the technological dimension. Investment decisions must be accurate in new technologies and they must be adaptable with them.

c. Socio-Cultural Dimension

Customs, morals, values, and demographic characteristics of the society in which the organization operates are what made up the socio-cultural dimension of the general environment. It indicates the products, services, and standards of conduct that society is likely to value and appreciate. The standard of business conduct varies from culture to culture and so does the taste and necessity of products and services.

d. Politico-Legal Dimension

The politico-legal dimension of the general environment refers to the governing law of business, business-government relationship, and overall political and legal situation of a country. Business laws of a country set the do and don'ts of an organization. A good business-government relationship is essential to the economy and most importantly for the business.

e. International Dimension

Today the Global Society concept has brought all the nations together and with the modern network of communication and transportation technology, almost every part of the world is connected. Virtually every organization is affected by the international dimension

MCQ – Factors Affecting Decision Making

"It is better to be approximately right than precisely wrong"

—Warren Buffet

To enhance your understanding of the factors influencing decision making, try out a small exercise:

1. If two executives deal with the same subject at the same time yet interpret it differently, the factors responsible for their dissimilar perceptions reside in:

    a. The target being perceived.
    b. The timing.
    c. The context of the situation in which the perception is made
    d. The perceiver.

2. Which one of the following is not a factor that influences perception?

   a. target
   b. society
   c. perceiver
   d. situation

3. Personal characteristics of the individual perceiver include all of the following except:

   a. His/her attitudes.
   b. Personality.
   c. Expectations.
   d. Location.

4. The focus of a person's attention appears to be influenced by:

   a. Interests.
   b. Past experiences.
   c. Expectations.
   d. All of the above

5. _____ allows us to "speed-read" others, but not without the risk of drawing an inaccurate picture.

   a. Selective perception
   b. Memorization
   c. Mental desensitization
   d. Periodic listening

6. Most interviewers' decisions change very little after the first _____ minutes of the interview.

   a. 1-2
   b. 4-5
   c. 30-40
   d. 50-60

7. The optimizing decision-maker is:

   a. Rational.
   b. Creative.
   c. Satisfying.
   d. Innovative.

8. Decision making is initiated by:

   a. A problem.
   b. A solution.
   c. Conflict.
   d. Perceptual distortion.

9. Rationality assumes:

   a. High intelligence.
   b. Consistency.
   c. Maturity.
   d. Unlimited choices.

10. Which is not one of the steps in the rational decision-making model?

    a. Defining the problem
    b. Identifying the decision criteria
    c. Rating the alternatives
    d. Computing the decisions that satisfy all

11. Research on what game has provided an excellent example of how intuition works?

    a. Soccer
    b. Chess
    c. Cricket
    d. Badminton

12. Business students, lower-level managers, and top executives tend to score highest in the _____ style of decision making.

    a. Analytic
    b. Directive
    c. Conceptual
    d. Behavioral

13. Your experience tells you that this project has merit. You decide to use _____ decision making and continue the project.

    a. Compulsive
    b. Intuitive
    c. Rational
    d. Satisficing

14. Which of the following is not an organizational constraint on decision making?

    a. Performance evaluation
    b. Reward system
    c. Personality
    d. Formal regulations

15. _____ refers to the seriousness of a problem's effect

    a. Urgency
    b. Impact
    c. Growth tendency
    d. None of the above

Answers: 1(d), 2(b), 3(d), 4(d), 5(a), 6(b), 7(a), 8(a), 9(b), 10(d), 11(b), 12(a), 13(b), 14(c), 15(b).

CHAPTER 13

Project Contracts and Common Allegations

"Lost time is never found again."
— Benjamin Franklin

"A project" is a discrete set of inter-related work activities constrained by a specific scope, budget, and schedule to deliver, performed in a logical sequence to attain a specific result and achieve the strategic goals of an organization. Each activity, and the entire project, has a '**Start and Finish date**'.

Going by the above definition, the entire project has a start and finish date but in the case of most of the PSEs, both the dates are very difficult to adhere to. The **start date** gets off the mark due to delay in decision making at the time of finalization of contracts as for such high-value projects considerable time is taken to finalize the vendor/contractors because decision-makers always want to appear fair and transparent at each step because of "perceived risks" in the decision being taken. It is a fact that such high-value projects are always under the scanner of investigating agencies.

Further, during the execution of projects, many decisions are required to be taken due to site conditions, operational challenges, changed requirements, other constraints, and "Change Order" needs to be placed on contractors which again require decision making at various levels thus resulting in delays. Such delays in decision making during the commissioning of projects have made a major dent in the profits of many organizations.

Most of the delays due to "perceived risks" can be minimized if the following strategies are adopted while finalizing the tenders for such contracts and during the execution of the projects.

At the time of tender finalization, do a thorough check on the legal background of the party, its existing commitments, and obligations with their other clients, and the impact that a new agreement would have on them. Check that the persons attending the meeting have the authority to make final decisions and also clarify the authority from your end when specific questions to be answered.

Leverage your contract management systems to customize contract lifecycle to the specific needs of the contractual relationship and determine Key Performance Measures & Key Performance Indicators. Take time during the kick-off meeting to mutually agree on the length of review periods. Make sure to hold parties liable for timely revision and indicate that additional review time will affect subsequent processes and deadlines.

Make sure that the other party is aware of the consequences that delays have on your organization. Therefore, the scope statement should include specific clauses that provide details about change requests. For example, what can be defined as a change request, applicable cost ranges, how change requests are processed, and how changes would affect existing timelines?

Convene a meeting between the department doing the contract management work and those impacted by the process. Discuss the timelines agreed with the contractor and support required from various agencies. Further, members of the department responsible for contract management should be trained in the Company's contract management process, terms used, and guidelines for the function. Please keep complete contract addendums, noting any changes in the contractual agreement.

A study undertaken by Vigilance indicated various aberrations in the finalization and execution of contracts as mentioned hereunder:

Common Allegations

- Favoritism
- Award of contract to favored firm bypassing more deserving lower tenderer/s on flimsy grounds
- Award of contract at exorbitant rates
- Execution of Substandard work
- Acceptance of Substandard Supplies
- Overpayment/Payment of work not done
- Failure to Carryout out Quality Check
- Misappropriation of material by the contractor in connivance with officials.

Execution of Contracts

- Failure to incorporate accepted tender conditions in contract agreement
- Introduction of condition(s) having financial implications
- Change in specifications during execution
- Altering the location or nature of work giving undue advantage to the tenderer
- Unreasonable Variations in terms of
    - Quantity
    - Items
- Introduction of New Non Schedule Items
- Transportations from much higher lead than intended in the tender
- Acceptance of material of inferior brand then specified in Contract Agreement

- Acceptance of under specification work or supply
- Not following laid down procedure
- Bypassing certain processes
- Not conducting requisite tests
- Use of un-approved raw materials

Payments

- A temporary overpayment in Running Bills
- Payment in anticipation of work to be done or supply to made
- Final overpayment
- Payment for the services not rendered
- Inflated measurement
- Multiple measurements

CHAPTER 14

Indenting/Tendering & Common Irregularities

"Coming together is beginning. Keeping together is progress. Working together is success"

— Henry Ford

The starting point of any procurement for material/services is to raise indent/purchase requisition. Although unfortunate, but it is a fact that in case of any complaint/scrutiny relating to the award of tender/contract for procurement, the first person questioned is the user/indenter, and if any irregularity is observed, he is taken to task. Generally, in PSEs, the user is a technical person and may not be aware of procedure/guidelines in this regard as he is always busy with his day to day routine jobs which generally require his technical acumen.

Whereas, procurement being the commercial issue, it requires Commercial Acumen to which he is never exposed. Further, the indenter is required to prepare a judicious estimate for the procurement being made and it becomes a highly challenging job for him as he is not aware of the current market i.e. availability of vendors and prevailing prices. Thus, he generally depends on the last prices obtained for the item/services and adds variation assuming the inflation.

Guidelines for raising the indents/purchase requisitions, preparation of estimates, scrutiny, and action on indents are therefore prepared by every organization.

A study undertaken by Vigilance indicated various aberrations in the indenting process as mentioned hereunder:

Justification of Quantity

- Excess quantity is projected over and above actual consumption pattern
- Quantities (items) procured on the early delivery basis but not consumed as stated in the indent.
- No justification is given for sudden jumps in quantity projected in the current year vis-à-vis consumption in the previous year
- For regular consumption items, projecting quantity for more than a year's consumption
- Splitting up of quantities for the same item(s) into separate smaller value indents
- Mix-up of matching/non-matching items in the same indent.

Eligibility Criteria

- Mentioning of earliest delivery dates as a prerequisite even where not required
- For major equipment supply – mentioning the execution of orders for same/similar item on a value basis rather than the capacity basis
- For item supply – not mentioning the minimum quantity of same material supplied to other firms
- Mentioning steel plant experience for jobs of general nature
- The clear cut-off date for successful operation/experience not indicated

- Specifying fixed turnover criteria in enquiry even when a lesser number of items are allowed to be quoted
- Experience of – repaired or new construction — not specified
- Experience of a particular operation for multi-use products is found quite restrictive e.g. in case of pumps, compressors, etc
- Documentation required for acceptance/eligibility is not specified.

Specifications

- Sometimes made either too restrictive considering functional end-use & availability in market or based on old/obsolete models/technology
- Mentioning a particular brand name in Limited Tender Enquiries (LTE)/Open Tenders (OTE)
- Mixing-up of BIS/other standards with own specifications
- Parameters specified are not matching with technology specified
- Mentioning of special features of equipment of a particular manufacturer in LTE/OTE
- Old specifications mentioned even after amendment in BIS/ASTM, etc
- New item specification is made on the lines of budgetary offer from a single firm.

Preparation of Estimate

- Based on the old Last Purchase Price (LPP) for items being procured after a long gap
- Budgetary quotation obtained only from one source
- An estimate is based on a previous order placed on a single tender basis

- The estimate is prepared considering branded products but specifications are kept generalized
- Where +/- limits over Last Purchase Price (LPP) mentioned – not backed up with proper data/justification.

Acceptance/Rejection Criteria

- Critical parameters are not identified. In some cases, parameters that are difficult to measure are indicated
- Range/tolerance limits are not provided in specifications
- Ambiguity in rejection criteria and penalties to be imposed
- Time limits for replacement of rejected material not specified

Tendering

The next most important step in procurement is tendering. Tendering should be done to ensure the procurement of material/services maintaining Economy, Efficiency, Fairness, and Transparency. It is, therefore, necessary that Notice Inviting Tenders (NIT)/Request for Quote (RFQ) must be issued with due care and diligence. It should be ensured that Eligibility Criteria should be neither too stringent to restrict competition nor relaxed resulting in procuring inferior quality material/services. Special care is required for procuring material on the Repeat Orders/Emergency/Single Tender basis.

Generally, in most organizations, we attach standard general instructions to tenderers. However, extra care is required while stipulating Special Instructions to bidders as it will become the criteria for acceptance/rejection of tenders during techno-commercial evaluation. Some important points to be kept in mind while drafting special conditions can be as under:

- Site visits, if required, should be mentioned along with the location of the site.
- The payment terms should be specified.
- The conditions for off-grade/rejection of the supplies should be specified.
- The Eligibility Certificate and documents in support for the same to be stipulated.
- Documents in support of financial positions need to be specified.
- Statutory obligations on part of the bidder should be unambiguously mentioned.
- The type/number of equipment along with the ownership requirements should be specified.
- The evaluation criteria of the offers with all factors for loading to be specified.
- The Executing Official for the contract to be specified, preferably by name.
- Security Deposit, Mobilization advance, and their modes of payment/recovery to be stipulated.
- Integrity Pact, if applicable in your organization must be sent along with tender and it should be mentioned that tenders received without duly signed IP shall be treated as invalid.

Let's look at some of the common irregularities observed during scrutiny/investigation in a different mode of tendering:-

Open Tenders

- Inadequate Notice
- Inadequate Time available for participation
- Inadequate Publicity

- Late availability of Tender Form, Drawing, etc.
- No publicity to Corrigendum issued. Tender Opening Date (TOD) extension.
- Issue of tender form denied on the pretext of Non-fulfillment of eligibility criteria.

Limited Tenders

- Arbitrary selection of firms
- Firms with better experience ignored and firms with dubious credential selected
- The inadequate time is given for participation in the tender
- Tender Notice not sent to all the firms
- Bogus firms selected to inflate the number
- Cartelization by the firms
- No checks on quotes by sister concerns against one enquiry.

Single Tenders

- Projecting undue/artificial urgency
- Selecting unsuitable tenderer based on exaggerated credentials, ignoring his past failures
- Accepting exorbitant rates on the grounds of urgency then merrily giving extensions with a token penalty or without penalty
- Procuring material as proprietary whereas other vendors available.

General

- Twisting, Suppression, exaggeration, Manipulation, and Half truth by Tender Committee or TEC.
- Depict better-placed bidder as unsuitable or less suitable
- Exaggerating track record of the favorite bidder

- Suppression/downplaying his past failures
- Exaggerating past failures of his main rival
- Ignoring/Suppressing otherwise satisfactory credentials of the main rival
- Projecting the lowest rates of the main rival as 'unworkable' based on the exaggerated estimated cost
- Projecting undue/artificial urgency and then bypassing lowest offer on the ground that agency has some other works on hand
- Manipulating technical aspects to reject inconvenient bids on artificial grounds.

CHAPTER 15

Decision Making – Case Studies

"Good judgment comes from experience and experience comes from bad judgment"

You will be required to show ***courage*** in each of the decisions you are going to take in the following case-lets basing it on your ***conviction*** that the decision you are going to take is "the best" under the prevailing situation and circumstances. This conviction will be based on your ***competence*** in two areas, first your knowledge of the subject including your commercial acumen, and second, your understanding of the rules, procedures, guidelines, or even customaries of your organization in dealing with such situations. Please be ***committed*** to taking your decision before reading the rationale for the correct decision

Let's understand that customaries or practices are respected not only by audit or vigilance but even by other investigating authorities e.g. CBI provided that these customaries are still prevailing in the organization and not yet replaced by any written rule, procedure, or guideline. However, the responsibility of satisfying the authorities shall lie on the shoulders of the concerned executive to convince the agency that this is a custom or practice in your organization by showing records of such similar decisions taken in the past based on the same practices.

Last but not the least, your commitment towards your job, duties, and responsibilities will be the deciding factor to perceive your intentions i.e. either the decision taken was in the right earnest or not.

In the instant case of taking decisions on the cases mentioned in this book, it may so happen that you may avoid breaking your head and wasting your time in deciding on the issue which may not be concerning you at the moment and may rather prefer to read the book further to know the rationale behind the correct decision. Fine, nothing wrong with it, but it will show a lack of your commitment.

Let us try and understand the importance of rules/procedures/guidelines and also rationality in decision making through these small-small case-lets. I endeavor to convince the reader that rules, procedures, and guidelines prevailing in our organizations are enablers in decision making and have been carefully drafted to ensure the safety of the organization as well as our safety and peace of mind.

To facilitate you in decision making, let's assume that all other issues related to the case have been checked and found to be in order and you have to decide only on the issue which is in front of you. Please write your decision in the blank space given under the situation before proceeding further so also mentioning the rationale behind your decision.

It will help you in understanding the nuances in the decision-making process in the public sector scenario. Before proceeding further, let me once again request you to please try and give your answer after analyzing the situation.

By three methods we may learn wisdom: First, by reflection, which is noblest; second, by imitation, which is easiest; and third by experience, which is the bitterest. – Confucius

Case No. 1

As Head of Marketing Department, you are worried about poor sales during the year and a huge inventory of finished products lying in your warehouse. You have received a Letter of Credit (L/C) for Rs. 5 Crores from a customer on 30th March for sale of material which is lying in stocks for around 10 months. You advised your Finance Manager to get the L/C checked and obtain confirmation. He informed that L/C is in order but obtaining confirmation may take one/two days as he has to check from issuing as well as controlling office of the bank as per stipulated guidelines about acceptance of Letter of Credits/Bank Guarantees and Banks were closed on 31st March. You are in no mood to forego sales during the year. You advised your Senior Marketing Executive to personally go to the issuing office and obtain confirmation, which he brought in writing from the issuing office of the Bank and also satisfied himself by discussing the matter with the concerned Branch Manager of the Bank.

Whether, you will advise finance to issue a Delivery Order which will result in increasing sales by Rs. 5 crores and clearing your slow-moving stocks during the year itself, or wait for finance to complete the formalities, which may result in losing sales and adding up inventory. It may not be out of place to mention here that it is your experience in the past that getting confirmation from the Controlling Office of the bank is a mere formality as in 100% earlier cases you found the L/C or BG was found to be in order.

Ans._____

_____

During my sessions, the reply I received from most of the participants was that they will advise finance to issue a delivery order. Further, your decision-making will be the result of your perception that seeking confirmation from the controlling office of the bank is a mere formality as till now you have never faced a problem with the instrument once confirmed by the issuing office.

If your reply is also the same nothing to worry about, you have done a good job by securing higher sales and clearing your old stocks, except for the following problem.

When you sent the documents to the bank for getting payment, the Branch Manager was on leave and the Assistant Branch Manager refused the payment stating that although L/C is genuine but signed by an executive who has the authority to issue such letters of credit up to Rs. 50 lacs only. Now, what will be your next course of action?

You will rush to the controlling office of the Bank i.e. their Zonal/Regional office. You will discuss the matter with the Zonal Manager and after seeking the details from his office, if he alleges that your employee in connivance with the branch manager of the concerned bank branch has committed the crime. Maybe you will feel offended and seek the details for such a serious allegation. He will easily convince you that you have always used their bank guarantees and letter of credits after seeking confirmation from the controlling office. Then, why in this case, established practice was not followed. His perception may be that your employee was involved in the crime. At the most, he may assure you to take action against the Branch Manager but shall regret the inability to make payment.

Heavens will fall on your head! You and your team have been leveled with a serious allegation only for deviating from the laid down guidelines regarding seeking confirmation from issuing as well as controlling office of the bank before further action.

To date also, many scams are getting unearthed relating to irregularities/ fraud by banks/with banks. To keep you and the organization safe and secure from such frauds, if a guideline has been issued to double-check the veracity of the instrument i.e. Bank Guarantees/Letter of Credits, etc. is there anything wrong with these guidelines. Do these guidelines exist to keep you safe or they are hindrances to your effective decision making?

This is a real case where the material was sold against the Letter of Credit. The Branch Manager of the Bank who signed the L/C and also issued the confirmation letter was on leave on the day when documents were presented to the bank for payment. Assistant Branch Manager advised officials of the Selling Company to contact the controlling office of the Bank. Upon inquiry about the genuineness of the L/C, he commented that L/C is genuine but regretted his inability to make payment.

The officials immediately rushed to the Controlling office of the bank and showed the documents to the Regional Manager of the bank stating that the payment has been refused by the concerned branch. They were shocked to hear when the Regional Manager after seeing the Letter of Credit told that the payment, in this case, is not possible. He informed that though the L/C is genuine, however, the Branch Manager of the Bank who signed this L/C is having powers to sign such documents up to Rs. 50 lacs only. On inquiry as to how we are aware of powers of your executives, RM alleged that it appears your officials are in connivance with our Bank Executive otherwise you would have sought confirmation from us as was done in all previous cases and called for old records and showed where confirmation was sought from controlling office before accepting such documents.

Till now, you were celebrating for higher sales so also for liquidating your old stocks, but, now it was the time to secure your payment which was not forthcoming and chances of recovery appeared negligible.

During the further inquiry, it was found out that the branch manager of the concerned bank was in connivance with the customer and they were very much aware that they will not be making any payment for the material they are lifting from you.

The Marketing Head and Finance In-charge of the Company were penalized in the case not for putting Company to a loss of Rs. 5 crores but only for violating the laid down procedure concerning the acceptance of such L/Cs for not obtaining the confirmation from Controlling Office of the issuing bank.

It will not be fair if I don't tell you the fate of the money blocked in the above case. The Company could realize the principal amount after two years with the help of the Reserve Bank of India. Although FIR was also lodged against the branch manager of the bank and the customer for the forgery, I am not aware of the outcome of the case.

Case No. 2

Your sister plant is sending you special steel slabs on an Inter Plant Transfer (IPT) basis which is your raw material for further rolling of special steel Coils and sheets. However, due to breaking down in their plant, they could not supply you the required Slabs as per schedule whereas you have committed delivery schedule for the supply of finished steel to your valued customers. Thus, you decided to procure the same from private parties in the country who are manufacturing these special steel Slabs. You invited bids from 3 reputed manufacturers on Limited Tender Enquiry (LTE) basis for procuring 1500 MT special steel Slabs on 60 days credit basis. The L-1 rate received is Rs. 75000 per metric tonne, L-2 was Rs. 77000/-per tonne and L-3 was Rs. 78000 per tonne whereas your internal estimated price was Rs. 70000/- per tonne.

Purchase Department requested the L-1 party to reduce the prices through the mail but the party refused. However, after repeated requests and persuasion over the phone and through mail/fax, they agreed to reduce the price to Rs. 73000/- per tonne on an advance payment basis. However, this condition of advance payment was later removed by the supplier at the request of the Purchase Department. The purchase department has now sent you the file for justifying the reasonability of the L-1 rates as you are HOD of the Indenting Department and the estimate was prepared by your department.

What will be your stand concerning the reasonability of L-1 price? Please remember you require the material urgently otherwise your production may suffer and you may even lose the customers.

Ans._____

_____

Your obvious answer, in this case, shall be to go for procurement at Rs. 73,000/- pmt keeping in view the urgent requirement of the material. Further, the other two suppliers have quoted higher prices and thus the reasonability of the L-1 rates is also established.

Let's analyze the situation!

This is high-value procurement with an estimated value of Rs. 10.50 crores. As per procedure in many PSEs, for such high-value procurements, negotiations should be carried out by a duly constituted committee consisting of members from the Purchase Department, Indenting Department, and Finance Department across the table and not by a person/department as was done in this case. Thus, this will be looked at as a violation of the stipulated guidelines and concerned executives may face the wrath of vigilance/other investigating agencies.

Even if we look into the case from a commercial angle, negotiation across the table is essential for this high-value procurement as negotiation is a process that requires both skill and competence. If you are agreeing to buy the Slabs at Rs. 73000/- pmt, you are bringing on record that your estimate was incorrect. Whereas, it may be possible that although your estimate was correct but identified suppliers may be aware that you are in urgent need of material, and in their urge to exploit your urgency, they would have raised their margin i.e. jacked up their quoted prices.

Negotiations as done in this case can't be termed as negotiation as this is only bargaining. Whereas negotiation is a process which requires a deeper understanding of the subject i.e. lot of homework is required to be done before reaching the negotiation table and different people inducted in the committee may have different competencies and skill, thus, the joint result will always be better than individual bargaining. Negotiation is a four-step process consisting of first, Preparation i.e. homework, second, Argument i.e. discussions across the table to understand each other's viewpoint on the subject, third is Proposal, where you propose your intent again here, comes the LIM objectives i.e. What you will like the most from this negotiation, Intent is that you should get minimum this much discount (in case of PSEs i.e. this is the deviation range acceptable from the quoted prices as per procedure in vogue to get the proposal through from Competent Authority without much hassle) and Must is the last limit i.e. beyond which the price shall not be acceptable to you. Last but not least is Bargaining where you close the deal and agree/disagree with the final proposal keeping in view your LIM (Like, Intent, Must) objectives.

It is my experience that in PSEs, negotiation is taken as a ritual to seek some discount whereas suppliers are well equipped to face such negotiations and they come to the negotiation table after a lot of homework i.e. after working on strengths and weaknesses of their opponents as well as their own.

I have personally experienced in many cases that in PSEs, we generally start negotiation with the threatening that we may go for re-tendering if the supplier doesn't agree to our request for reducing the rates. On the other hand, suppliers due to their long association with these organizations are very much aware that re-tendering may not be feasible for them because of their long tendering process. Thus, their opening dialogue will be, Sir, inadvertently we have quoted very low price and we shall be grateful if you kindly help us in getting out of this tender. Now, you are left with no other alternative but to beg for some discount and after a lot of persuasions, they may offer you some discount in the name of maintaining the relationship with the Company and that too after putting many conditions e.g. to help them in getting expeditious payment of their pending bills, leverage in the delivery period, etc. etc.

Again, this a real case with some more inputs where 8 senior officials of a steel plant along with the supplier were booked for putting the company to a loss in connivance with the supplier. The FIR was lodged by CBI and the premises of these officials were raided by CBI. However, when they were framing the charges against the officials of the steel plant, they felt the need for getting clarity on the purchase procedure of the company as many references were found made in the records seized by CBI about the purchase procedure.

CBI decided to seek the help of the vigilance department of the company to get clarity on the procedural issues. A communication was received by the vigilance department of the company from CBI to depute an official to the CBI office who is well versed in the purchase procedures of the company. Accordingly, as the author was the official who was looking after purchase procedures, was sent on tour to the concerned CBI office.

The challenge, in this case, was that neither the company nor the concerned officer was aware of the case and the only document he carried with him was a copy of the purchase procedure of the Company.

During deliberations with the concerned CBI official, who was also the investigating officer of the case, it was felt that CBI is interpreting the purchase procedure in a police language whereas it was a commercial document. CBI officials also got convinced that their perception in the case was based on their interpretation of the procedure, whereas facts were different from what they perceived. He was a very nice and open-minded police officer; he suggested taking the statement of vigilance official to keep it on records. As the vigilance official was confident about his deposition, he also agreed. After two days of deliberations and discussing all the relevant points where police interpretation was different from the commercial interpretation of the purchase procedure, I came back to my office.

It was after around six months, I was delighted to know that all the eight steel plant officials were exonerated in the case by CBI recommending Regular Departmental Action (RDA) by the Company only against the Head of Purchase Department for deviating from the laid down procedure relating to negotiation as discussed above. It further strengthened my belief in the rules/procedures and guidelines of the Company.

Case No. 3

You are a large manufacturing company with a large set up of branches and stockyards in different cities of the country. You have floated a tender for the award of Handling Contract tender with an estimated value of Rs. 10 crores per annum for 4 years duration from the date of award of contract on the open tender basis for handling iron and steel materials in one of your stockyards. Bidder is required to possess at least 10 cranes of different capacity either in the name of the company, partner, or proprietor. As per tender conditions, techno-commercially eligible bidders shall be required to show original documents for equipment owned by them as stipulated in their tender documents. You have received 7 bids and during the techno-commercial evaluation, only 4 bidders viz. A, B, C & D were found eligible. It was observed during scrutiny of documents that two parties (let's say A and C) have submitted an identical list of equipment owned by them in their tender documents but meeting the requirement of ownership as stipulated in terms and conditions of the tender.

You requested all the four eligible bidders to produce original documents for verification as stipulated in the tender terms and conditions. However, only three parties (A, B & D) presented the original documents for equipment owned by them for verification as stipulated in the tender conditions and the documents were found in order. Third-party C who submitted the identical list of documents as mentioned above has not produced the original documents for verification despite repeated reminders. As you can't wait indefinitely, you have to proceed further with the tender finalization. What will be your stand in the case i.e. whether you will reject the bid of the bidder C who has not shown the original documents as stipulated in the tender conditions or accept their bid?

Ans._____

_____

The obvious answer in the instant case is that you will reject the bid of the party who failed to produce original documents for verification as stipulated in the tender terms and conditions otherwise it may be viewed as a violation of stipulated tender terms and conditions. Why I am telling it so confidently because in almost 100% of cases, whenever I asked this question, the reply was that his bid shall be rejected.

Let's analyze the situation:

You have already seen the original documents produced by bidder A and in case of the other party C, who has submitted the identical list of equipment but not producing the original documents for verification, may be intentionally trying to get his bid rejected in the process. The fact is that even if they would have produced the documents, the documents shall be the same which you have already seen and found them to be in order. Thus, it can be concluded that you have seen the original documents for a list of equipment possessed by them for both parties A & C, however, only once. Do you need to see the same original documents again!

It happened in a case, where after techno-commercial evaluation of the offers, the three bids were rejected as they were found not meeting the required eligibility criteria. Out of 4 bids found eligible, two were belonging to sister concerns and one out of their two bids was rejected due to the inability of the party to produce original documents for verification.

The price-bids of 3 parties were opened and party A emerged as the lowest bidder at say Rs. 83/- per metric tonne (mt) for the handling of iron and steel materials in one of the stockyards of a big steel manufacturer.

However, due to a complaint made by one of the bidder alleging other irregularities, all the records about this tender were scrutinized by the vigilance department. During scrutiny, this fact came to the notice of investigating agencies that the bid of Party C has been rejected for his inability to produce documents for verification as stipulated in tender terms and conditions.

Although the tendering process was found followed as per the laid down procedure and there were no other discrepancies observed in this case. However, Vigilance Department advised to cancel the tender and go for re-tendering stating that the original documents were seen by the evaluation committee for both parties A and C in one go as they submitted the identical list. However, no action was taken against any official as they were found following the stipulated tender conditions.

Surprisingly, in the re-tendering, the lowest rates received were say Rs. 45/- pmt quoted by the other party as against Rs. 83/- pmt received in the earlier tender. It was revealed later that party A and C who were sister concerns, submitted two bids, one with higher rates and one with competitive rates but when they found that their real competitors were out during techno-commercial evaluation, they got their bid with lower rates rejected by not showing the documents as required as per tender terms and conditions and grabbing the contract at higher rates.

Case No. 4

As Head of Works, you could finalize the tender for the award of re-building contract for coke oven battery no. 1 of your plant in around six months from the date of opening of the tender with great difficulty seeking validity extension of tenders for further three months as they were originally valid for 90 days only. However, out of the three techno-commercially eligible bidders, L-1 backed out when the order was finally released on him stating that the validity of my offer has expired yesterday. However, the L-2 bidder has offered to do the job at L-1 rates and on the same rates, terms, and conditions.

Since the nature of the job is urgent and considerable time has already been lost in the finalization of the tender, whether you will award the job to L-2 at L-1 rates. Please note that the L-2 party is also a renowned contractor and in your opinion, they are even better than the L-1 as you had seen their performance earlier and found them very efficient.

What will be your decision in the case i.e. whether you will award the job to an L-2 contractor on the same rates, terms, and conditions to take up the long-overdue job or go for re-tendering?

You are aware that in your organization, tendering is a time-consuming process and your production is suffering for want of capital repairs.

Ans._____

_____

Since considerable time has already been lost in the tendering process and the circumstances of the case, you may be thinking to award the job to an L-2 contractor at L-1 rates as he is also a renowned contractor, and re-tendering shall be a time-consuming process. Further, the expeditious capital repairs shall help you in boosting your productivity. You may even be considering negotiating the rates with the L-2 party as he has now become the lowest bidder after the withdrawal of the bid by the L-1 party.

If you are thinking like this, you are not wrong as many executives in the public sector even at very senior positions were also of the same opinion when this case was discussed with them.

Let's analyze the situation:

Before we discuss the CVC stand on such matters, please consider if L-3 offers to do the job at a price lower by Rs. 50 lacs than L-1 price, will you award the job to L-2 or L-3 as he is also techno-commercially eligible bidder. It may result in negotiation with L-2 & L-3 which are not allowed in the Public Sector.

Central Vigilance Commission has a very clear view on the subject and it is reiterated time and again starting from CVC Order Nol. 98/ORD/1, which states as under:

"Some of the organizations have sought clarification as to whether they can consider the L-2 offer or negotiate with that firm if L-1 withdraws his offer before the work order is placed, or before the supply or execution of work order takes place. In this regard, it is clarified that such a situation may be avoided if a two-bid system is followed (techno-commercial) so that proper assessment of the offers are made before the award of work order., Therefore, if the L-1 party backs out, there should be retendering transparently and fairly. The authority may in such a situation call for limited or short notice tender if so justified in the interest of work and decide based on the lowest tender."

Central Vigilance Commission again vide their Office Order No. 68/10/05 directed that in case of L-1 backing out there should be re-tendering as per extant instructions. Vide Circular No. 4/3/07 it was reiterated that in case of L-1 backs-out, there should be a re-tender. Therefore, in such an event, where L-1 is backing out for any reason whatsoever, there should be re-tendering of the case.

Case No. 5

In the above case, if it is decided to go for re-tendering, whether you will allow L-1 to quote against the fresh tender for the same scope of work.

Ans._____
_____

After going through the guidelines issued by CVC concerning treatment with the backed out bidder, you may be thinking to de-bar him from re-tendering. Emotionally also you are hurt as for the delay of only one day, L-1 bidder has wasted your hard work done in six months. Thus, your reply will be "no" to his participation in the re-tendering in the same case. You may be thinking to ban him for other tenders also for some time.

Let's analyze the situation:

Kindly reconsider your decision as this is not a case of backing out by the L-1 bidder. Instead, he has only informed you that his bid is no longer valid on the day of issuance of Work Order. He may be willing to participate in the re-tendering at the current rates. Thus, keep your emotions away and allow him to re-tendering.

Case No. 6

Your Company has decided to appoint a Consultancy Agency for undertaking Employees Engagement Survey and suggesting methods for re-deployment, development, and proper engagement of employees. You selected the four best agencies that are competent to undertake such work and invited quotes from them after finalizing the terms and conditions of the tender by obtaining EOI and preparing an estimate based on the budgetary quote received from one of the selected party. The budgetary quote was Rs. 1.05 Crores whereas the L-1 rates discovered through Reverse Price Auction (RA) is only Rs. 20 lacs.

You have observed that all four parties participated in the RA and around 85 times bidding was made by these parties. Incidentally, the budgetary quote was received from the same party who has emerged as the L-1 bidder. L-2, L-3 & L-4 were Rs. 23 lacs, Rs. 27 lacs and Rs. 31 lacs respectively. As Competent Authority, the file is with you for accepting the L-1 bid or for re-tender.

What will be your decision in the case? Please note that you can't take a Performance Guarantee Bond from the L-1 bidder as such condition was inadvertently not incorporated in the NIT although you generally insist on performance guarantee bonds from such bidders who are quoting abnormally low rates.

Ans._____

Your reply most probably shall be to go for re-tender because of the difference of more than 500% in the L-1 price and the estimated price. Further, the quality of the job can't be guaranteed as the provision of taking Performance Guarantee bond doesn't exist in this tender.

You may be correct in your decision making but think of only one question, what will be the estimate for the next tender? If you keep it again Rs. 1 crore, the question shall be asked that when you are aware of market price, why such a high estimate? If you keep the estimate at Rs. 20 lacs i.e. the lowest price received in this tender, a question may be asked that if your estimate is Rs. 20 lacs and somebody was ready to work at this price, why you have not offered him the job?

Let's analyze the situation!

Decision making is always based on the information available to you for taking a rational and logical decision. In this instant case, you have invited the four best consultants available in the country for the job; the price has been discovered through Reverse Auction after 85 times bidding that shows intense competition amongst the bidders. The difference between L-1 and L-2 bidder is only Rs. 3 lacs. Moreover, the difference between L-2 and L-3 bidder again is only Rs. 4 lacs and the highest price quoted is Rs. 31 lacs. Thus, none of the bidders is anywhere near your estimate. Thus, the L-1 price obtained appears to be the real market price for the job envisaged.

This case-let is based on real experience. Training institute of one Maharatna PSU was looking for a Consultant who could do an Assessment of their senior officers to facilitate the company to understand their developmental needs for future growth. Since this was a job envisaged for the first time, it took a lot of time to finalize the terms and conditions of the tender as the understanding scope of work was in itself a challenging job. However, after great efforts, a tender was prepared after obtaining a budgetary quote from one of the reputed consultants. However, what happened during price-discovery has been elaborated above.

The Head of the training institute discussed the matter with his Senior Faculty Member dealing with commercial acumen who had joined the institute a few days back only and on his request handed over the file to him. My experience says that in such cases, your advice should also be based on facts and not your opinion in the case.

After going through the file, the next day he discussed the matter with the Head of the institute and convinced him that he could go ahead with the tendering process. The Head is also well-versed with the purchase/contract procedure of the company, immediately queried as to whether the lowest bidder will be required to give the bank guarantee for Rs. 80 lacs. The experienced Faculty informed him that the Performance Guarantee was not possible in the case as it was inadvertently not mentioned in the tender terms and conditions. The Head got tensed again fearing that all his efforts would go in vain! But the faculty member was confident that this case could be processed further for approval of top management and made a draft note for his perusal which was to be given by the committee of indenters. Incidentally, the indenter was a committee of three faculty members, and one more faculty member was included by reconstituting the committee.

It was a small note recommending the award of the job to an L-1 bidder containing the following information:

1. Re-confirmation has been sought from the lowest bidder that he has understood the scope of the work and he shall abide by all our terms and conditions.
2. The lowest bidder is a reputed consultant and he has successfully completed this type of Assessment work for some other PSUs.
3. The rates have been discovered through Reverse Auction where intense competition was observed amongst the parties as evident from 85-time bidding.
4. the difference between L-1 & L-2 is only Rs. 3 lacs, incidentally the difference between L-2 & L-3 is only Rs. 4 lacs, etc. thus the L-1 price appears to the market price for the job envisaged.

Given the above, the Committee recommends awarding the job to M/s. XYZ on the L-1 rates quoted by the party.

After perusal of the note, the first reaction of the Head of the Institute was that was no mention of estimate in the note. To which it was informed that the estimate was to start the job and now when actual market rates are available from the best Consultants, what was the need for mentioning the estimate. Believe me, the note was received duly approved by the institute within 7 days after approval of Director (Pers.), Director (Finance) and Chairman of the Company.

For the benefit of readers, let me explain the price discovery process through Reverse Auction. There is Forward Auction (when you are selling the goods) and Reverse Auction (when you are buying the goods/services). This process of price discovery entails the use of IT, as after the techno-commercial evaluation of the bids, a user-id and password are given to all techno-commercial bidders by the IT agency engaged to conduct e-auction and all bidders are required to log in into the system on a given date and time.

After logging on with their user-id and password, a template appears on the computer screen with a Start Bid Price (SBP). This SBP is nothing but the estimate and various organizations are using different methods for fixing start bid price as per their prevailing procedure/guidelines. Bidders are free to quote any price (generally less than the estimate), the moment any bidder quotes his price, the SBP is out and his price appears on the screen. Please note, only the quoted price appears and not the name of the bidder. Other bidders are free to quote their price and bidding continues within the allocated time. However, if any bidder revises the price when only one minute is left for the auction to close, what will happen? The other bidders will still get an opportunity to quote their price within the next five minutes. An indication shall appear on the screen that the bidder has to decide within the allocated time otherwise the price appearing on the screen shall be taken as the lowest price obtained. This cycle continues till there is no bid for continuous five minutes (or the time decided by the organization) and after the grace time is over, the last price appearing on the screen is taken as L-1 price.

In the case of Forward Auction, a similar method is followed except the Start Bid Price is generally the floor price fixed by the organization, and bidders are required to quote their highest price.

Case No. 7

Your plant is generally producing 60000 MT of Ferro Silicon/Ferro Manganese during the year although it can produce up to 100000 MT. This material is used by your sister plants. You have been advised to produce 90000 MT Ferro Silicon/Ferro Manganese during this year keeping in view the huge demand for these material projected by your sister plants given their increased production targets as finalized in the Annual Business Plan meeting. Your plant is capable of producing this quantity but you are dependent on one raw material supplier with whom you are having an MOU for the supply of 60000 MT Manganese Ore during the year on a pro-rata supply basis every month. He has expressed an inability to supply more than the MOU quantity during the year because of his prior commitments. Therefore, the plant is searching for another source of raw material supply to bridge the gap. However, nothing could be finalized although 4 months of the financial year have been passed. In the meantime, it was informed that one private party has imported the raw material and the ship is reaching Vizag Port tomorrow.

Your Chief Executive is having business relations with this party and requested them to give 10000 MT to your plant, if possible. Party has agreed to offer the same at the price which plant is paying for a similar quality of material to its regular supplier provided the order is placed on them within 24 hours as otherwise; they will shift the material to their factory to avoid port rent/charges. You may be aware that material once unloaded at the birth has to be cleared within the stipulated time to avoid heavy port rent. You are Head of Purchase Department and your Chief Executive has advised you to ensure issuance of PO within 24 hours as it is an emergency. Whether you will get the Purchase Order issued to the party within 24 hours or wait for the completion of formalities.

Ans._____

Keeping in view the fact that your plant is in dire need of raw material to fill the gap between raw material available and raw material required for meeting the production target, you will get the Purchase Order placed within 24 hours as it is a case of emergency procurement. Moreover, four months have already passed and there appears no scope for getting the raw material from any other source so quickly if we leave this opportunity. You will get the emergency indent raised and place the Purchase Order within the stipulated time given by the supplier.

Let's analyze the situation:

Your perception of the urgency/emergency may be correct. But it is your perception. Generally, to declare any procurement as emergency procurement, two conditions are required to be met. First, the material is not available in the plant, and second, the procurement is critical for the plant operations. In many organizations, the Head of Department of the concerned department/ unit has to give these two certificates to declare the procurement/contract as an emergency contract, one is called "Non-availability Certificate" and the other is called "Criticality Certificate".

Please think for a moment and decide whether these two certificates can be given by the department in this case. The fact is that the material is available in the plant, though less than the required quantity to meet the enhanced production target. The procurement is not critical to the plant as the plant is not closed or going to be close due to the non-availability of raw material.

When we are taking such decisions, we have to keep in mind others' perspectives also. This is a high-value purchase from a private party where so many other conditions have to be checked e.g. expenses at the port, transportation, security of material at the port, and quality of material (supplier has informed about the similar quality and not the same). Further, the price quoted by the party may be similar to the price we are paying for the raw material being procured from the indigenous source but what about other expenses that will add to the cost of procurement.

Moreover, this is single tender non-proprietary high-value procurement; full justification shall be required for obtaining approval of the Chief Executive.

Proprietary purchase is for the item manufactured by only one manufacturer, where you have no choice but to purchase the same from the sole manufacturer. However, a single tender non-proprietary purchase is one where you are selecting a party on a nomination basis although other techno-commercially eligible bidders may also be available.

This question has been asked many times to participants of the Decision-Making Programme, whether "Godrej furniture" can be procured as a proprietary purchase? Give yourself a minute and reply giving your reasons.

Going by the definition given above of proprietary purchase, please think whether the furniture is being manufactured by only "Godrej" and you will get the reply.

In many organizations, for single tender non-proprietary cases, approval of the Chief Executive is required irrespective of the value. During deliberations on the issue, I found that many officials are very critical on the issue because, in their opinion, it at times deprives them of procuring the best quality material. While I appreciate their concern, still reiterate that complete justification is required for procuring material on a nomination basis especially in public sector undertakings for the reason mentioned below.

According to Article 14 of the Constitution of India, "the State shall not deny to any person equality before the law which means equality to status and of opportunity."

While procuring items/services on a single tender nomination basis, are we not denying opportunity to others who may be eligible to apply? Thus, it will be a violation of the constitutional right of individuals. However, under exceptional circumstances or inevitable situations, such procurement is allowed with the approval of the Chief Executive to protect the interest of the Organization.

Last but not the least, always keep in mind that these two words appear similar "Urgency" and "Emergency" when we perceive the situation but they are two different words, and both the situations are required to be dealt with separately. In most of the public sector organizations, officials are given full liberty to take decisions to mitigate emergency but no such relaxation is provided in rules/procedures for meeting urgency. You may think about why this difference in dealing with two situations appears the same. It is because emergencies can't be foreseen although you may take measures to mitigate emergency as and when arises. However, urgency is a result of negligence on the part of the concerned official as he has not taken action in time which resulted in this situation of urgency or at times may create a situation of "emergency" but that emergency shall also be treated as "created emergency". You will be able to appreciate this difference between urgency and emergency through the next case.

Case No. 8

You are Head of Works of your plant and you received a call from your night shift in-charge of your rolling mill department at around 1.30 am that one critical bearing has suddenly broken and production has come to stand still and this bearing is not available in the department. You put everybody on the job immediately to search for the bearing to re-start the production and rushed to the plant. It is observed that this is a special bearing and not used by other shops/departments of your plant and is not available anywhere in the plant. Daily production loss is envisaged at approximately Rs. 5 crores per day. On the second day, your Purchase Officer found that this bearing is available with only one supplier which he has procured for some other party but willing to offer it to your plant at Rs. 2 crores. The last purchase price of this bearing was Rs. 50 lacs. Purchase Officer has taken the requisite certificates from the HOD of the department that the bearing is not available in the plant and procurement of bearing is very critical as the plant is suffering production loss. Purchase Officer has put up the proposal for procuring this bearing on an emergency basis and the file has come to you for approval. What will be your decision in the case?

Ans._____
_____

Your obvious reply shall be to approve the proposal since it is an emergency and both the conditions of "non-availability" and "criticality" have been met. The fact is that your plant has already suffered a loss of around Rs. 10 crores and any delay in procurement shall add to your losses.

Let's analyze the situation:

The decision appears perfectly in order. During my vigilance tenure, I had handled a similar case where someone complained to CVC against the Head of Purchase Department that he had procured this bearing at exorbitantly higher prices from a known supplier with malafide intentions. However, when the case was investigated, things were found in order as it was a case of real emergency procurement. Thus, the vigilance department recommended closure of the case to CVC after obtaining approval of the Chief Vigilance Officer.

One small query was raised by CVC before giving their advice in the case. They enquired when the bearing was so critical why the same was not kept in stock to avoid production loss and such an emergency.

The query was forwarded to the concerned department for their reply. The department replied that they raised the indent for procurement of this bearing around 6 months back and the file was shuttling between them, finance, and purchase department for around 3 months for want of clarifications, etc. The file is lying with the Purchase Department for the last 3 months. They gave date-wise records to substantiate their claim. It was found that the duly approved indent was lying with the purchase department for more than 3 months without any action.

The clarification received from the concerned department was forwarded to the Central Vigilance Commission. CVC concluded this case as a case of "Created Emergency" and recommended penal action against the Head of Purchase Department.

This word created emergency was heard by us in the vigilance department for the first time. Chief Vigilance Officer advised us to initiate a study on delay in procurement by the Purchase Department. Surprisingly, many indents were found lying with them for more than a year also.

Case No. 9

Your office has invited bids for finalization of conversion arrangement for Thermo Mechanically Treated (TMT) bars FE 600 grade in 18mm to 22mm size (finished product) from Billets (semi-finished product) to be supplied by you. It has been mentioned in the tender documents that the facilities offered by the party shall be thoroughly inspected before finalization of the contract. You received five bids, out of which two were rejected during techno-commercial evaluation. You advised the other three parties that you will carry out inspection of 22mm TMT rolling in FE-600 grade on the stipulated date and time and asked parties to confirm. Two parties agreed for inspection on the stipulated date but one party demanded inspection of 20mm TMT rolling. On your insistence to inspect only 22 mm rolling (it being a non-standard size and to be used for critical purposes e.g. roof bolting in underground mines i.e. to save precious human lives), party again insisted for inspection of any other size except 22mm stating that they do not have any order for 22mm TMT and shall not be in a position to get rolling of 22mm TMT inspected. What will be your stand in the case i.e. whether you will accept party's request or reject his bid.

Ans._____

_____

Most probably, your reply will be to reject the bid of the party who has expressed his inability to show rolling of 22 mm TMT as it is a non-standard size and critical for the operations it is used. Further, it is a question of the safety of human lives who are working in underground mines.

Let's analyze the situation:

Your perception of looking at the issue may be correct, but procedurally it may not be correct to reject the bid of the party as inspection criteria in Notice Inviting Tender (NIT) stipulated that "the facilities offered by the party shall be thoroughly inspected before finalization of the contract." Is there any mention of the inspection of specific rolling of 22mm TMT i.e. this specific size in the tender documents?

Please keep in mind that the tender document is the only source of communication between you and the bidder and take out this wrong notion from your mind that it is your tender and you may ask for anything you wish from the bidder, of course, to protect the interest of the Organization. It is your document so long tender is not issued but once issued it becomes legal and binding on both the parties i.e. seller and the buyer to abide by the terms and conditions of the contract. Acceptance or Rejection of the bid has to be only as per the criteria mentioned in the tender documents.

It is observed in many cases of the public sector tendering that it takes a lot of time during tender evaluation and organizations keep asking for much information/documents/certificates which were not mentioned in the tender to come to a judicious decision of accepting or rejecting the bid. It may appear appropriate to ask for such documents in the interest of the procurement/ job envisaged but it is highly risky to accept or reject the bid based on such documents/criteria which were not mentioned in the tender documents or terms and conditions.

It is once again reiterated that acceptance or rejection of the bid can be within the criteria mentioned in the tender. Therefore, preparation of tender documents especially eligibility criteria, technical and commercial terms have to be carefully drafted and approval of Competent Authority may be obtained before the issuance of tender. Generally, tenders are prepared on a cut, copy, and paste basis which creates a lot of problems during the evaluation of the bids received. The preparation of tender documents in the Public Sector is done by one executive in Purchase Department whereas techno-commercial evaluation is generally done by a committee consisting of senior officials from various departments e.g. Technical, Purchase, and Finance.

Case No. 10

You are Chief Executive of M/s. ABC Ltd. manufactures Ferro-silicon and Ferro-Manganese. An open tender for procurement of 20000 MT Charcoal was invited by your plant. The major technical specifications found mentioned in the tender were as under:

a. Carbon content in the charcoal should be a minimum of 70%.
b. Moisture content in the charcoal should be a maximum of 10%.

It was further mentioned in the tender that suitable penalties shall be deducted for Carbon if less than 70% and moisture if more than 10%.

7 bids were received against the tender and 5 parties offered material as per tendered specification but two parties offered material with carbon minimum 75% and moisture maximum 5%. All the seven parties were declared techno-commercially eligible by Tender Committee and price-bids were opened. The party who offered material as per tendered specification emerged L-1 and was recommended for award of the tender. However, when the file was sent to Head of Finance for his concurrence before your approval as Chief Executive, he observed that there is a difference of only Rs. 100/- pmt between the party who emerged L-1 and offered material with Carbon (minimum) - 70% and moisture (maximum) - 10% and L-2 party who offered Carbon (minimum) - 75% and moisture (maximum) - 5%. Simple mathematical calculations proved that your plant could have saved a huge amount if the tender documents were prepared correctly adding a bonus for supplying material with better specifications. However, since everything else was found in order, he gave his concurrence to the proposal for your approval.

The file is with you for approval. What will be your decision in the matter i.e. whether you will approve the file or advise re-tender with correct specifications i.e. adding bonus and penalties both instead of the only penalty?

Ans._____

_____

Your answer most probably shall be to go for re-tendering with revised specifications. It appears logical also as the loss appears visible in the decision if you approve the file for placement of the order on the Lowest bidder. Further, the relation of Finance Associate with decision-maker in the Public Sector is like his Consultant on financial matters and generally, decisions are taken in consultation with finance. Once your consultant has brought out such a big anomaly in the tender terms, it appears most appropriate to go for re-tendering with revised terms and conditions.

Let us check the calculations as to how he has arrived at the loss of Rs. 2.80 crores. Let's assume the L-1 price as Rs. 15000/- pmt. Thus, for 20000 MT, the purchase value shall be Rs. 30 crores. Suppose L-2 price is Rs. 15,100/-pmt. Therefore, the purchase value in this case shall be Rs. 30.20 Crores. You will be paying Rs. 20 lacs more but shall be required to procure 2000 MT less Charcoal. How?

Charcoal is procured for extracting carbon out of it. If you are getting 5% extra carbon from the supplier i.e. coal with 75% carbon, you will require 1000 mt less material. Similarly, if the moisture content in the charcoal supplied is 5% instead of 10% there will be a saving of 1000 mt. Therefore, for extracting the same amount of Carbon, you will be requiring 18000 mt Charcoal only instead of 20000 mt. Simple, Isn't it?

Let's analyze the situation:

The only problem is the party that has emerged as the L-1 bidder. Suppose he complains to CBI that although he is meeting all the techno-commercial terms and conditions of the tender and has emerged as an L-1 bidder still the tender has been canceled with dubious intentions.

How will you save yourself? Your calculations! However, the investigating agency may ask you whether the party who has emerged as L-1 was within your tendered specifications, yes or no, we know that our answer will be YES. They may ask, you finalized the specifications, why you have not checked such calculations at the time of floating the tender. Even if it was an inadvertent error at the time of finalizing tendered specifications, the techno-commercial evaluation was done by the technocrats of your plant, why they had not pointed out this major flaw in the tender before recommending for the opening of price bids. Do you have any satisfactory reply to these queries? Thus, they may allege that when the price has been discovered and your favored has not emerged as L-1, you have intentionally rejected the bid of the lowest bidder with mala fide intentions and gone for re-tendering. Whatever the agency is alleging is based on the facts except for your intentions which are not visible as it is a matter of perception. Since the investigating agency is viewing the total process as per their perspective (based on the complainant's perception) and responsibility is now on your shoulders to convince them about your intentions i.e. your perception of looking at things. You will be running from pillar to post to justify your action.

Please note that the reason for re-tendering after the opening of the price-bids should be attributable to price only and nothing else because price-bids of only techno-commercial bidders are opened. After the techno-commercial evaluation is over, there is no scope left for any technical/commercial consideration, especially after price bid opening. Thus, in the instant case, canceling the tender on technical grounds after the opening of price-bids is not advisable.

Senior officials of one Public Sector undertaking are facing CBI wrath for the above decision to go for re-tendering although in their opinion it was the best decision to avoid a visible loss to Company. However, CBI has charged them for willful rejection of L-1 bid as price-bids were opened after due diligence i.e. techno-commercial evaluation of the bids and bid of L-1 bidder was found eligible.

Case No. 11

Due to a severe recession and sluggish demand in the domestic market, your Company is finding it difficult to sell its products in the country. The prices offered by customers are much below your expectations. You are manufacturing steel products in an integrated steel plant on a 24x7 basis. Thus, you can't cut production. It was, therefore, decided to book export orders for your major product to be supplied in the next few months so that you can reduce the supply of your product in the domestic market to contain the falling prices.

International markets were also not very upbeat and with a lot of efforts, you could book orders for 3000 MT & 3200 MT @ USD 300 pmt for the European market. In the meantime, you received an enquiry for a supply of 20000 MT for the same product from the Singapore party.

After protracted negotiations, the party agreed to pay USD 280 pmt for an entire lot of 20000 MT, which was to be supplied within four months. The rate offered by the party, although low, is almost at par with the international market rates and forecast for future rates as available from various bulletins.

Whether you will approve the deal at USD 280 pmt?

Ans._____

_____

If you are an analytical type of executive, you may not accept the order as the financial implication between two export orders booked in the same month shall be around Rs. 2.40 crores. (Simple calculation 20000x20x60(exchange rate of USD Vs. Rupee). Further, the material has to be supplied within four months and assumptions about future trends are based on the forecast.

You may be correct in your assumptions but the whole trade is based on the forecast. Further, the rates can be compared between the same or similar size of packages. Thus, rates for a package of 20000 MT cannot be compared with a package of 3000-3200 MT. If you decide not to book the order today and the market further goes down, you may not get this deal tomorrow. As per the age-old economic principle, prices are governed by demand and supply. By restricting the supply of this product in the domestic market, your sales realization may improve. However, it will be difficult to quantify the gains as the same will be based on forecast only. Thus, you should approve the deal.

Case No. 12

In the above case, let's assume that after booking the export order at USD 280 per tonne for the export of 20,000 tonnes of HR Coils, the domestic market started improving. On the day of actual dispatch of export of 20000 MT of material four months after the date of the contract, there was a difference of Rs. 6000/- pmt between the listed price of the product and the contracted price. Whether you will still go ahead with the dispatch or cancel the contract.

Ans._____

_____

The loss in this deal shall be approximately Rs. 12 crores, therefore, many of you may like to get out of the deal and cancel the contract.

Let's analyze the situation:

Your decision may appear correct as you are trying to avoid the visible loss of Rs. 12 crores to your organization. However, please remember that contracts are legally enforceable and once concluded should be honored. Even otherwise also, no one will like to do business with you if you are not a committed supplier.

It reminds me of a similar case, where someone complained to CVC, CBI and CMD of your Company that Executive Director (Export) has put the Company to a loss of Rs. 12 crores stating facts of the case i.e. you booked an order for such huge package at the prices lower than prevailing international prices and for supplies after four months. As the complaint addressed to Chairman of the Company was forwarded by him to Chief Vigilance Officer, he got the case investigated. It was observed in the case that the order was booked as per laid down guidelines and customaries prevailing in their export department. Customaries are practices being followed over a while. They are accepted not only by vigilance but CBI also. However, the onus of proving that this is customary i.e. a practice that is uniformly followed in many other cases lies on the executing authority.

Before I proceed further let us understand what exactly it means by custom or practice through a small story.

In one village, there was a ritual to give the sacrifice of a goat on a particular day in a year at a designated place and it was festival time for villagers in not only that village but also for surrounding villages as many shopkeepers were putting up their stalls, etc. A 12-year-old boy went to see the ritual with his father and found that one gentleman was standing at the sacrifice place with both hands up in the air as if he is holding something. The boy enquired about the same from his father as to why this gentleman was standing like this? His father replied, it is customary and he is seeing one man standing in the same position every year since his childhood. The boy was not satisfied with the reply and again asked his father for the reason. His father pacified him by saying that he should enquire the same from his grandfather as he was not aware as to why the gentleman was standing in that position at the sacrifice place. After reaching home, the boy rushed to his grand-father and fired his question. His grand-father took some time to traverse to his memories and suddenly he got the reply. He explained that at the designated place where the sacrifice is being given, there was a big Banyan tree, and once it happened that while the ritual was being performed, the sword touched the branch of the tree and the sacrifice got spoiled. Since then, duty was assigned to one gentleman to hold the branch up at the time of sacrifice. Although the tree has fallen long back the customary is being followed every year to avoid any obstruction to the sacrifice.

I hope you have clearly understood the meaning of the customary or practice.

As everything was found in the case in order, the vigilance department recommended for the closure of the case, and the report was sent to CVC. After a thorough examination of the case, CVC closed the case.

After about six months, one senior official of the CBI called the concerned vigilance official who investigated the case requesting for his help as they were not aware of the international trade and terms used in international trade. I don't know where they got the information about the concerned vigilance official of the Company, but that's their job.

On reaching the CBI office, the vigilance official was escorted to the office of the concerned Superintendent of Police, CBI where five other persons were sitting and discussing the case and three of them were in police uniform. After the exchange of pleasantries, the first question was asked by a gentleman in uniform about the correctness of the figure about loss i.e. whether there was a loss of Rs. 12 crores to the Company. The obvious answer by the official of the Company was "YES", the figure is correct. The moment he told yes, all the officials of CBI present in the room stood up saying that you have still closed the case. The vigilance official got nervous but stood by his stand that the figure is correct but it is a business loss. Thereafter, it followed the detailed deliberation on the guidelines, forecast, and also on customaries being followed in finalizing such cases. This went on for hours and after satisfying themselves about the system of order booking, SP, CBI enquired as to why Company had not canceled the deal when such huge loss was evident on the day of dispatch. It was explained to him that in business, contracts are honored, otherwise who will come for business with us tomorrow. Vigilance officer of the Company, who was facing CBI wrath for hours, also got the courage to say, Sir, if there would have been a loss to the customer, whether he could cancel the cancel. The immediate reply of SP, CBI was this is not possible in business as he has already entered into a contract. To which vigilance officer told in a lighter vein that since he is representing Public Sector Company, he is being asked so many questions as to why the deal was not canceled whereas on the other hand, you are telling, canceling the contract is not possible in a business. This statement though told casually during discussions but had a great impact on CBI officials. SP, CBI was a nice and generous officer, he told the Investigating Officer to recommend closure of the case.

The intention behind explaining the case is to give confidence to decision-makers in Public Sector that commercial decisions may go haywire as they are based on the forecast and nobody can see the future except God, thus the decision making shall always be based on the perceptions which must be backed by the facts, data, and forecasts. Be brave in taking commercial decisions but ensuring compliance with laid-down procedures/guidelines and/or practices.

Case No. 13

You had floated an open tender for procurement and installation of critical spares in your plant at an estimated cost of Rs. 1.40 crores giving four weeks for submission of bids. Five bidders submitted their bids and after techno-commercial evaluation by the duly constituted committee, which took two months for evaluation, only three bidders were found meeting your eligibility criteria. One of the conditions for eligibility was relating to the experience of the bidder in executing the same job in other reputed company/public sector. The bidder was required to submit an experience certificate in this regard. (It was mentioned in the tender documents that the certificate has to be obtained from the Company on their letterhead and to be submitted in original along with tender).

Price-bids of the bidders who were found techno-commercially eligible were opened on the stipulated date and time in presence of bidders. Party ABC Ltd. was found the lowest bidder followed by the party XYZ Ltd. as the L-2 bidder.

However, after the opening of price-bids, M/s. XYZ complained that ABC Ltd. has never done the job envisaged in this tender and they have submitted the forged certificate.

On inquiry, it was found that the experience certificate submitted by M/s. ABC Ltd. was forged as the issuing company denied in writing that he has ever issued such a certificate to M/s. ABC Ltd.

As per the prevailing purchase/contract procedure in your company, there is a provision for such eventualities. As per the laid down procedure - "If any adverse report is received against the party on an investigation or otherwise during the processing of the tender, such tender should be rejected. It is further mentioned in the procedure that even if such a report is received after the opening of the price bids, then also the quotation/tender of that tenderer shall be rejected after recording the reason with the approval of the Competent Authority.

You are the Competent Authority for finalization of the tender, what will be your stand in the case i.e. whether you will go for re-tender or shall proceed with the tender after rejecting the bid of M/s. ABC Ltd. (Please note you shall be left with only two eligible bids in that case, which is allowed as per your procedure but with the approval of your Chief Executive).

Ans._____

I have got so many different responses against this case (some out of the box) that I am not sure what will be your response in the case. However, my stand in the case is very clear.

Let's analyze the situation:

In the instant case, it is evident that the bidder has committed a crime by submitting the forged certificate, thus his bid has to be treated as invalid. Once you treat his bid as invalid, you are left with two valid bids to proceed further with the tendering process and that's allowed as per your procedure. It is not a case where L-2 is becoming L-1 after the rejection of the invalid bid, but it has to be treated as a case, where you received only two valid bids and the procedure in vogue for dealing with such a case has to be followed i.e. approval of Chief Executive has to be obtained for further processing of the case in case there are only two valid and eligible bids at the time of price bid opening. You may proceed with the finalization of the tender if the same is permitted by the Competent Authority.

Further, as M/s. ABC Limited has committed a crime; you must lodge FIR with the police authorities as per law of the land.

Case No. 14

There are four registered vendors for the supply of a particular type of pump to your plant. However, two more local dealers have contacted your office for the supply of these pumps at a very competitive price and they are found representing the reputed manufacturers of such pumps. As per the laid down procedure of your company, you can resort to a limited tender enquiry by registering the parties on a provisional basis, if you do not have sufficient registered parties. As HOD, Will you allow these two manufacturers also to participate in the Limited Tender Enquiry to invite more competition?

Ans._____

_____

Your obvious answer in the instant case shall be "yes", we must allow these two manufacturers also by provisionally registering them as it is helping in more competition i.e. getting competitive bids.

Let's analyze the situation:

You may be correct in your approach but here is a problem.

Why these two manufacturers only who approached you through local dealers? There may be many other pump manufacturers who have not contacted you as they may be waiting for registration to open i.e. your seeking applications for fresh registration. If your answer is to increase the competition, the best and the most transparent option is to go for open tendering. Why you have not resorted to open tender?

For the sake of more clarity, think of a situation that one more reputed manufacturer who was looking for an opportunity to enter into business with you got to know that you have allowed two new manufacturers in your limited tender enquiry although they were not registered. He has complained to your vigilance department that if I would have been aware that my company will also get an opportunity to bid had I met the concerned official and pleased him. What will be your stand in the case in that case?

Do you want to land yourself into such an awkward situation even when you intend to increase the competition? Your reply can be that your procedure allows you to go for provisional registration and you have followed the laid down procedure. Right! But it says that you can provisionally register the parties if you do not have sufficient registered parties for the items you wish to procure on a limited tender enquiry basis.

Are four sufficient or not? Further, who will decide? It has been deliberated above that vigilance functions on "Preponderance of Probability". Thus, it will be the prerogative of the investigating officer in the case and not yours.

Case No. 15

You are Project Manager of your Company and in the on-going modernization work in your plant, the contractor sought time extension to complete the job stating that he could not complete the work in time as there was inordinate delay in handing over the site to him by the plant authorities, which was a fact. Further, a considerable delay was observed in handing over the drawings/designs, etc. to the contractor. However, you are aware that there were delays from the contractor's side also in arranging man/material/machinery from his side. You are also aware, that any dispute at this stage regarding the imposition of penalty/LD may result in further delaying the project and the contractor may stop the work if you impose a penalty, which you cannot afford at this juncture. Please keep in mind that records of such delays from either side have not been kept ready and it will take time to fix the responsibilities. Whether you will accept the request for time extension as sought by the Contractor, keeping the decision of imposition of L/D in abeyance?

Ans._____

_____

Your obvious reply shall be to get the job done first and later decide the issue relating to delay analysis, calculation of Liquidated Damages (LD) and levying penalty, etc. It appears a logical decision as any dispute with the contractor at this stage may result in further delays thus putting the company to further loss.

Your decision to keep the disputed issue of levying LD appears reasonable because as Project Manager your topmost priority is to get the project completed at the earliest possible time. You are aware of the fact that any dispute with the contractor at this stage may result in a stoppage of work.

Let's analyze the situation:

During an intensive examination of the projects, it was observed that most of the Project Managers do make a decision that you have taken in the instant case. However, it was observed during an investigation of the records at a later date that due to an inordinate time-gap between the commissioning of the project and preparation of delay analysis report, etc. it becomes extremely difficult to find out the extent of delay on the part of the contractor. As this issue is required to be sorted out before issuing the Final Acceptance Certificate (FAC) to the contractor, it delays the issuance of FAC. In fact, in many cases, FAC could not be issued even after many years of commissioning of the project for want of details relating to the recovery of Liquidated Damages. This ultimately results in disputes and thus arbitration. The arbitration proceedings not only result in a waste of valuable time of concerned executives but most of the time it also results in loss to the Company as we could not exhibit records of delay attributable to contractors to honorable arbitrators during arbitration proceedings, thus resulting in an arbitration award in favor of contractors.

I am sure, if you go through the records in your Organisation, you will find an inordinate delay in issuance of Final Acceptance Certificates and it may not be surprising if you find that many FACs are yet to be issued for projects completed years ago.

Thus, the correct decision at that stage shall be to allow time extension for completion of the work in writing stipulating that this is "without prejudice" to your rights to recover liquidated damages and other penalties, etc.

Case No. 16

You have invited open tenders for a project where the estimated value of the project is 200 crores. As per terms of the tender, the sole bidder, consortium, and joint ventures are allowed to participate in the tender. It is also mentioned in the terms and conditions of the tender that eligible bidders shall be allowed to change the composition or constitution of the consortium if they so desire.

When you are in the process of evaluating the bids, one bidder has requested you to allow them to change the composition of their consortium. Whether you will allow them?

Ans._____

_____

The answer, in this case, is very simple, as the terms of tender allow the bidder to change the composition or constitution of the consortium, if they so desire, you will allow them to change the composition of the consortium.

Further, your decision to allow change is perceived by the fact that if they change the composition of the consortium at a later date, you have to re-check their eligibility, etc.

Let's analyze this decision!

In this case, I wish to draw your attention to the word "eligible bidder" as the tender terms stipulate that eligible bidders shall be allowed to change the composition/constitution of the consortium. The eligibility of the bidder is yet to be checked. The bidder is not yet declared techno-commercially eligible. Therefore, at this stage, it is not possible to consider his request for a change in the composition of the consortium.

As regards your perception relating to allowing change at a later date after completing the techno-commercial evaluation, it is a fact that his eligibility has been decided based on the constitution and composition of consortium members, their technical/financial status, etc. and any change after the finalization of eligibility shall add to extra work.

Please consider if you allow such changes at the evaluation stage itself, any bidder shall give you bid by adding names of consortium members who are readily available but may not be technically suitable to you as he knows at a later date before his bid is rejected, he shall be allowed to change the composition or constitution of the consortium. Do you want this to happen with your tender?

I kept on reiterating during my interactions with the participants that business communication is an art that has to be learned by each executive. Again the challenge in most of the PSUs is that they hire engineers and not managers i.e. executives are neither trained in the art of business communication by their respective academic institutions nor by the Organizations. However, their career paths require them to prove at every stage that they ensure fairness and transparency in decision making.

The transparency will come only when we know what to communicate and how to communicate. Based on my experience of looking at the records from the other end i.e. during the investigation of the case, my perception is that most PSU executives lack communication skills. Therefore, even if they decided in the right earnest, it appears dubious to investigating agencies, and any explanation or clarification at a later date is taken as an "afterthought". Remember the quote of Dr. John Lund, I mentioned earlier:

"Don't communicate to be understood; rather, communicate so as not to be misunderstood."

This is expected during communication from all the PSE executives as their decision shall be examined by third agencies as explained above and they may not be aware of the background of the case. They have to make their judgment based on their perception which shall be formed after going through the records generated during the decision-making process. Further, the more threatening thing is that they start their investigation after going through the complainant version of the case, which has portrayed the decision-maker most negatively.

We have discussed above effective business communication. Always remember that the investigating agency is influenced by the version of the complainant which has been portrayed in his complaint thus perceives the decision in the same manner. You must keep the records in such a manner that you can influence his perception to help him to arrive at the correct conclusion in the case.

Case No. 17

You have floated a tender for civil works with an estimated value of Rs. 50 crores and financial eligibility criteria stipulate that bidder should have experience of successfully completing similar work for another PSU in the last 5 years amounting to not less than Rs. 5 crores in a single work order. The bidder was required to submit a copy of the work order and completion certificate along with the bid.

You received five bids and during the techno-commercial evaluation, it was observed that one bidder has submitted a copy of the work order amounting to Rs. 6 crores for successfully completing such a job for another PSU in a single work order along with a completion certificate. It was, however, observed that material i.e. Steel and Cement amounting to Rs. 2.50 crores was supplied by the PSU free of cost to the bidder as was found mentioned in the work order. Whether you will accept or reject his bid.

Ans._____

_____

Keeping in view the fact that the bidder has attached a copy of a work order of another PSU for total work amounting to Rs. 6 crores as stipulated in the tender terms and conditions, you will accept his bid. The total value of work executed by the bidder is Rs. 6 crores as against the eligibility criteria of Rs. 5 crores, what if it included a free supply of Cement and Steel valuing Rs. 2.5 crores.

Let's analyze the situation:

Your decision in the matter is correct but only to the extent that bidder has experience of executing the job up to Rs. 6 crores. However, in the instant case, it was financial eligibility criteria i.e. you wanted to check the financial capability of the bidder through previous work executed by him. From the copy of the work order attached to the tender documents by the bidder, it revealed that his financial exposure in the contract was only worth Rs. 3.5 crores and not Rs. 5 crores as required by you.

At times, it appears that investigating agencies are raising trivial issues as your acceptance of the bid was to increase competition which is the essence of commercial acumen. However, have you ever thought that in case the job is awarded to him, he may not be able to perform satisfactorily for want of sufficient liquidity as he is financially not as capable as envisaged by you while finalizing financial eligibility criteria?

It may also happen that someone complains that in case you were ready to accept relaxed financial eligibility criteria, I would have also quoted. I refrained from bidding in this tender as I have not handled any work of Rs. 5 crores or more.

In the instant case, although his work experience can be of handling the job up to Rs. 6.5 crores but his financial capability appears only Rs. 3.50 crores as per the attached work order. Thus, his bid is liable to be rejected.

Case No. 18

You have awarded a contract amounting to Rs. 20 crores for Scientific Exploitation of coal at your collieries to L-1 bidder for two years from the date of Letter of Intent (LOI). As per the tender terms, the successful bidder was required to submit a security deposit of Rs. 50 lacs in the form of Demand Draft/Pay Order/Bank Guarantee within 15 days from the award of LOI. The contractor is working in your collieries in other areas also and his bills amounting to more than Rs. 1 crore is pending for payment. He has requested you to adjust the security deposit from his pending bills. What will be your stand in the case i.e. whether you will allow recovery of the security deposit from his pending bills or advise him to deposit the same by way of DD/PO/BG before awarding of Work Order as per tendered terms?

Ans._____
_____

You will not accept the request of the party to adjust Security Deposit from his bills pending with you for payment because as per tender terms and conditions, the party is required to submit Security Deposit before the award of the contract. A simple decision isn't it. You are following tendered terms and conditions, then what's the matter.

Let's analyze the situation:

Your decision appears correct and logical as per the tendered terms and conditions. However, I invite your attention to CVC guidelines enumerated above, wherein it was suggested that the manager should decide as if he is taking for his own affairs. In the instant case, bills amounting to Rs. 1 crores are lying pending with you for payment. You could not release the payment for one reason or the other but the fact can be ascertained whether the bills are payable and the amount due is more than Rs. 50 lacs. If this fact is verified by your Finance Department, then where is the problem? You are having money with you and it is a matter of book entry. Please do it and get the job started.

Case No. 19

There was an inordinate delay in supplying new uniforms to around 700 employees of your company due to a severe cash crunch. Unions have threatened to go on strike if the uniforms are not supplied immediately. In the meeting convened by Chief Executive, you as Head of Personnel of that unit were asked to arrange the uniforms for employees at the earliest possible.

You are aware that arranging the same through the Purchase Department shall delay the procurement as they have a set process to follow for such procurements. You are confident that your department is capable of handling this procurement as it is a non-technical simple procurement. Whether you will allow your office to make the expeditious procurement or you will advise the Purchase Department to undertake the job on an urgent basis although in that case, things may not be under your control.

Ans._____

_____

Keeping in view the fact that any further delay in procurement of uniform for employees may result in Industrial Relation (IR) problem and that the procurement is simple and can be handled by your department, most probably your answer will be to procure it through Personnel Department or emergency purchase.

Let's analyze the situation:

If you also thought like this, nothing wrong, but please consider whether it is a purchase tender i.e. procuring clothing material from the supplier or a job contract i.e. the supplier shall be required to measure each employee and make uniform fit to his size.

Even if you feel your department is capable of handling this job, please think of ways to call quotations i.e. on an open tender basis, Limited tender enquiry, or on a single tender nomination basis. If in your opinion, it is a small job, you can shortlist the cloth merchants of your city and go for limited tender enquiry, please elaborate on the eligibility criteria for selection.

Let's move ahead and consider that your department does the short-listing based on some criteria, here comes the challenge of finalizing the specification of clothing material i.e. the percentage of cotton, viscose, etc. Please keep in mind, as per CVC guidelines, asking for a sample for clothing material is not allowed at the tendering stage. However, it can be asked from a successful bidder for indeterminable parameters such as, shade/tone, size, make-up, feel, finish, and workmanship, before giving clearance.

For the time being, let's assume, your department has done this job also successfully, how you will ensure checking the tendered specifications during techno-commercial evaluation.

There will be a chain of never-ending processes that have to be followed as per laid down procedure and guidelines for procurement, which your department may not be aware of. For the sake of argument even if we consider that your department shall take guidance from the Purchase Department as and when required. Then, in that case, It's better than the Purchase Department to take up the job to do it expeditiously instead of your seeking advice now and then and delaying the procurement process.

Case No. 20

Your daughter is employed in the Consultancy firm who has also applied for an award of financial consultancy contract against the tender floated by your Company (although no way related to the type of work for which tender is floated). You, as Finance Head of the Company, are required to evaluate the bids received. What will be your stand in the case?

Ans._____

_____

The instant answer in the case which will come to your mind is that if your daughter is not related to the type of work for which tender is floated and also the fact that she is just an employee of the company who wishes to bid and your daughter has no role in the case, you will evaluate the bid as in any other case.

Let's analyze the situation:

Please think of a situation where the said company gets the tender as it emerged as the lowest bidder after you had followed the laid down procedure during the evaluation and processing of the case. At the same time, your daughter also gets a promotion/pay hike based on her merit and capabilities.

Someone has alleged in a complaint sent to investigating agencies that to further the interest of your daughter, you have favored the Company during the evaluation process. What will be your stand in the case?

The responsibility of proving your innocence shall be on your shoulders. It appears to be a simple case but it shall be a difficult job as this will be a case of "conflict of interests" as both facts in the complaint are correct and required to be verified.

Therefore, in most of the public sector undertakings, in their Conduct and Discipline rules, it is mentioned that:

"No employee shall in the discharge of his official duties deal with any matter or give or sanction any contract to any firm or any other person if any of his relatives are employed in that firm or under that person or if he or any of his relatives is interested in such matter or contract in any other matter. The employee shall refer every such matter or contract to his official superior and the matter of the contract shall thereafter be disposed of according to the instructions of the authority to which the reference is made."

It may look ridiculous to withdraw yourself from decision making in all such cases where your relative is involved (directly or indirectly) but always remember this clause is more protection for you than your Company.

Case No. 21

A Public Sector undertaking floated a tender for the award of contract for the electrical job which included the laying of underground cables, the supply of cables as per IS standards, and connecting the cables with their main electrical panel. The only eligibility criteria stipulated for the job was that contractor should have experience of doing the same/similar job for any PSU/Government undertaking in the last five years. The bidder was required to submit the certificate in original received from the department where he had successfully executed the same/similar job.

During the evaluation of the bids received, it was observed by the Techno-Commercial Evaluation Committee (TEC) that three bidders have submitted their bids along with the certificates from PSEs for the same/similar job done as envisaged in the tender conditions. The certificates were on the letter-heads of PSE for whom bidders have successfully done the job. The committee declared all the three bidders as eligible and the job was awarded to the lowest bidder. Whether evaluation by the TEC was correct?

Ans._____

_____

Your answer most probably shall be "YES" as Techno-Commercial Committee while evaluating the bids have gone through the experience certificates submitted by the parties. As the three bidders who were declared eligible had submitted the required certificate and the same were found attached in original which were on the letterheads of the issuing PSEs. Thus, the committee was right in their recommendations.

Let's analyze the situation.

It's a fact that the committee did their job diligently and recommended only those parties as eligible who submitted the required experience certificate in original. Thus, they were right in their approach. However, a complaint was received by the vigilance department that the lowest bidder who has been awarded the job has submitted a forged experience certificate.

The vigilance department requested the records from the concerned official and found the original letter of the PSU which was alleged to be forged. As the name of the issuing officer, his designation, address, etc. were available, a letter was sent by the vigilance department to the issuing official of that PSU requesting him to confirm that the said certificate was issued by him. The reply was received immediately from the concerned official of that PSU confirming that the letter was not issued by him and his signatures were forged. Moreover, he informed the Vigilance Department that the said job was never done in their company.

However, by the time it was concluded by Vigilance that the job which was awarded to the lowest bidder after he was declared eligible based on a forged experience certificate, he had already successfully executed around 70 percent of the envisaged job. This was not a case attracting vigilance angle as the decision to award the job was found taken based on recommendations of the Committee relying on the documents submitted by the bidders. As customarily, the veracity of the certificates was not found checked by their unit, it can't be concluded that the committee was wrong in giving their recommendations, thus no action was proposed against the committee members. Although it was not a case involving a vigilance angle, it was established that the party who is executing the job has submitted the forged certificate to get the job.

Suppose, you are head of the unit and you have received this advice from your vigilance department, what will be your further action in the matter?

The first alternative is to ask the party to immediately stop the work but what next? The other alternative is to allow the party to complete the balance job (which is less than 30% of the total job awarded to the party) and then contemplate further action. What is your decision on the matter?

Most probably, you will go for the second alternative i.e. you will allow the party to complete the remaining job then go for further action. The point here is what will be your further action?

As the submission of forged documents attracts a criminal angle, your next action shall be to file a First Information Report (FIR) with the concerned police authorities for forgery done by the party and wait for the outcome of the police investigation and final court verdict in the case.

Case No. 22

For capital repairs in your mill to be taken as per schedule, you being from the user department raised an indent for procuring 150 bearings urgently (to be delivered within 30 days). Purchase Department reverted to you after calling quotations on a Limited tender basis informing that out of 10 quotations received, only 3 have agreed to supply the bearings in 45 days from the date of order, 3 have asked for 60 days and balance 4 parties have asked for 90 days. They have sought your written advice on the delivery period to be agreed as price-bids of only those parties will be opened who are within the delivery period agreed by the indenter. What will be your decision on the matter?

Ans._____
_____

The most probable answer shall be to go for accepting bids from the bidders who have agreed to deliver the material in 45 days as it is closest to 30 days asked by you. It appears a reasonable decision when you perceive that any further delay in deliveries may affect your capital repairs.

Let's analyze the situation:

If you look at your decision from a commercial angle, you will find that by restricting participation to only three parties, you have agreed to reduce the competition by 70%. On further analysis, it may be asked to you, if you can wait for 15 more days then why can't wait for 30 days or 60 days. This will result in never-ending questions from investigating agencies as to when the capital repair was announced, when you decided the requirement of equipment/spares and when the indent was raised, why such squeezed delivery period was kept, etc. etc.

My perception of the issue is that we as an indenter are always concerned about the timely receipt of stores/spares, etc; therefore, they intentionally give a squeezed delivery period in our indents. It is seen during several vigilance investigations that items valuing crores of rupees are lying in stores for years, which were indented on an urgent basis with a very short delivery period. One complaint which I regularly received from operations/planning engineers during my interactions with them was that in case of any irregularity observed in the procurement, the first person to be accused is the indenter. I am sorry but it is a fact that the first person who shall be asked for clarifications in case of any allegation/complaint about irregularities in procurement shall be the indenter only as he has initiated the procurement process.

In Public Sector undertakings, we generally follow the vertical hierarchy, and therefore in case of any irregularity observed in procurement/contract, the first person responsible shall be the initiator and the last person accountable shall be the approving authority. It is, however, to be noted that during investigations, investigating authorities consider the initiator as the department and not the individual who is the first signatory. Therefore, it is of paramount importance that each executive who is signing on the proposal be it for procurement/contract or any other administrative matter, is responsible to ensure the correctness/genuineness of the facts incorporated in the proposal.

Recently, I was informed about a case of procurement of some imported spares amounting to Rs. 50 lacs only where CBI after investigations have recommended for prosecuting four engineers of an indenting department for the wrong estimate which was based on the budgetary quote. Those four engineers were Manager (Operations), who initiated the proposal, Assistant General Manager (Operations), Dy. General Manager (Operations) and General Manager (Operations) who signed on the proposal initiated by the Manager of their department without checking the veracity of the budgetary quote. It was concluded by the CBI that the budgetary quote obtained by the department was forged and none of the accused officials checked the genuineness of the budgetary quote. Further, the budgetary quote was not obtained in the manner as stipulated in the laid down procedure of the Company.

If this is the outcome of a case, where four senior officials of a public sector undertaking have been prosecuted only for not obtaining the budgetary quote in a manner as stipulated in the procedure, it again strengthens my belief in the importance of rules/procedures/guidelines issued by your organization from time to time. I once again reiterate that please look at these procedures/guidelines as your enablers instead of taking decisions based on your perceptions i.e. in this case, when I was interacting with the concerned officials, I was told that they were aware of the procedure of calling budgetary quote especially in case of a proprietary procurement but there was a fire hazard in their plant and they wanted to get these spares at the earliest possible time. Calling a budgetary quote from the supplier as stipulated in the procedure would have taken a very long time.

Were they working for their ulterior motives or the plant? The obvious answer shall be that all their efforts were to expedite the procurement process and instead of waiting for getting a quote directly from the overseas supplier, they took the help of their local agent which has put them in such a mess from where when they will come out, nobody knows.

Case No. 23

You have opened price-bids for procuring 150 bearings to be delivered within 45 days, as no bidder has agreed to match your delivery schedule of 30 days although you required the bearings immediately for capital repairs. You opened price-bid of only 3 parties out of 7 bids received, who have offered to deliver bearings within 45 days as indenter has agreed for a delivery period of 45 days. The following rates were found quoted by the bidders.

- Party A – Rs. 12,000/- each for 50 bearings with immediate delivery and Rs. 12, 500/- each for balance bearings.

- Party B – Rs. 12,200/- each for 150 bearings for delivery within 45 days
- Party C – Rs. 13,000/- each for 150 bearings for delivery within 45 days.

However, immediately after the opening of price-bids, party A has given in writing to voluntarily reduce his rates as Rs. 12,000/- each for all the bearings. Please rank the party as L-1, L-2, L-3.

Ans._____

_____

The most common answer received from my participants is Party A shall be declared as L-1. The justification is given also appears logical as Party A has agreed to offer all the bearings at Rs. 12000/- each which is the lowest price. Further, he is giving 50 bearings ex-stock i.e. immediate delivery, which will help you in starting your work.

Let's analyze the situation:

The only issue, in this case, is that the indenter has agreed to a delivery period of 45 days and he requires 150 bearings. Although, quotation of party A has quoted his price in parts, the weighted price of each bearing in his case shall be Rs. 12,333/- which is more than Rs. 12,000/-, thus Party B shall be declared lowest bidder (L-1) in this case.

As far as to question of Party A offering voluntary reduction in the prices i.e. making them lowest at Rs. 12,000/- each bearing is concerned, please note that as per CVC guidelines such voluntary reductions may be accepted only from the lowest bidder.

Many questions shall be coming to your mind as to why we should procure the bearings at Rs. 12,200/- when they are available at Rs. 12,000/- each from other suppliers. The answer is straight and simple. As per CVC guidelines, negotiation under exceptional circumstances is allowed with L-1. Here, it can be treated as a case of limited suppliers as you have already rejected quotes of four parties for not meeting your delivery criteria and left with only three parties. Out of these three parties, one who has quoted the lowest price(Party B), may be asked to reduce the prices at least to the extent which is available on records i.e. Rs. 12,000/-. There can be two possibilities, either he will reduce the price or do not reduce. If he reduces the price during negotiations, an order may be placed on this party, or else you have two options, one you may go for re-tendering on a limited enquiry basis within these 3 parties or place an order on Party-B.

Only for the sake of discussions, don't you agree that there may be a possibility of getting prices less than even Rs. 12,000/- during negotiations. Party A has voluntarily given you a reduction of Rs. 500/- each on his quoted prices. In case, you can negotiate with Party B to seek the same discount which has already been offered to you, the order price shall be Rs. 11,800/- each bearing. Which one is less!

We generally do not consider such possibilities during actual working as our mind is pre-occupied with so many other important work/exigencies. Please keep in mind that investigating agencies have the full time to think of all alternatives in the case which is assigned to them for investigation. You will be cornered during the investigation by them with their perception. The only challenge shall be you can't refute their hypothesis as you have not checked the same following laid down the process to prove their assumption wrong.

Case No. 24

Your Company has floated a tender for certain jobs to be outsourced in a critical area of the plant. The tender specifications and eligibility criteria were kept as advised by the executing authority to invite competition amongst capable parties. After techno-commercial evaluation, 3 out of 5 bidders were found meeting the required eligibility criteria. However, after the opening of the price-bids, it was informed by the executing authority that the party who has emerged as the lowest bidder may not be able to perform satisfactorily citing examples of a different outsourcing job where the party could not perform thus resulting in hindrances in production. They have vehemently opposed awarding the job to this party as the job is required to be carried out in the most sensitive area of the plant and may result in a stoppage of production. You are Head of Operations of your plant and the file is pending with you for approval. What will be your decision on the matter?

Ans._____

_____

Most probably your answer shall be to reject the bid of the party as you are concerned about production. Many of you may go for a softer option to go for re-tendering as you may not like to award the job to a party whose reputation is not good.

Let's analyze the situation.

The tender has been floated stipulating terms, conditions, and eligibility criteria as stipulated by the executing authority. During the techno-commercial evaluation of the bids received, the lowest bidder was found to meet all your tendered terms and conditions. The objection of the executing authority has been received only when the lowest bidder has been identified. They would have faced some problems when the same party was executing a job in their plant. However, in this tender, the job requirements are different and the eligibility criteria have been finalized based on the recommendations of the executing authority. At this stage, finding fault with the lowest bidder on the ground of his failure in another job may be seen as an afterthought and may invite a vigilance angle. Why? It is because any investigating agency may doubt your intentions e.g. you don't want to work with this party for vested interests.

As already explained in another case above, the eligibility and capability of the bidder have to be ascertained at the techno-commercial evaluation stage. There also, if the bidder is found to meeting all your requirements, you can't reject a bid on your perception i.e. he may not be able to perform! Acceptance or rejection of bid at that stage also is required to be within the boundaries of tender terms and conditions. However, after the opening of the price-bids i.e. declaring a party techno-commercially eligible after due scrutiny (price-bids are opened after techno-commercial evaluation) rejecting a party on the technical reasons shall be seen as misconduct on the part of the decision-maker. At this stage, the only reason for rejection can be price i.e. if the price is not acceptable being very high or very low as compared to your estimate, the justification can be given for the rejection of the tender repeat tender not the bid of the lowest bidder to invite fresh bids and if required, fresh tender with revised eligibility criteria.

Case No. 25

You are a member of the Tender Committee and your Company has invited bids for civil work in the hot zone area of your plant with the eligibility criteria that bidder should have successfully completed the same/similar job against the order received from any Government Department/Public Sector Undertaking. In response, you received five bids, amongst these two bidders A and B have submitted an experience certificate from a reputed PSU for successfully completing the required job. However, it was observed that party B was sub-contractor to party A for the job which was awarded to them by the Public Sector Undertaking and both have submitted the experience certificate for the same job. What will be your decision in the case concerning acceptance/rejection of their bids?

Ans._____

_____

Based on the responses, I generally received from the participants, your choice shall also be to make party A eligible and reject the bid of party B for the obvious reason that the order was placed by PSU on party A and as per your eligibility criteria, job executed should have been assigned by a Government Department/PSU.

Let's analyze the situation:

Your logic appears reasonable but here is a problem why In that case PSE issued a certificate to both the parties i.e. A & B for successful completion of the same job. Further, did your tender terms prohibit bids from sub-contractors? If no, what will be your basis for rejection of the bid of party B? You wanted a certificate from the bidding firm that he has successfully executed the job for a PSE for order received from PSE, which may not be direct to him but to his main contractor.

However, in that case, you may think that why party A should be made eligible if he has not executed the job himself. Here again, it is the language of your tendered eligibility criteria which stipulates that the bidder should have successfully completed the same/similar job against the order received from any Government Department/Public Sector Undertaking. Whether party A was not successful in executing the order received from a PSE. If your answer is yes, why should it not be made eligible?

One more question which may influence your decision making shall be the fact as to why the PSE gave successful completion certificate for one job to the two parties. You may find it very in-appropriate to issue such a certificate to two parties for the same job done. If this is vitiating your decision-making process, please think of both parties A and B and try to answer a simple question. Whether both were successful in executing the order placed by PSU or not?

Party A was successful in executing the order placed by PSU by getting the job done through his sub-contractor. The responsibility of successful execution was on party A which he performed to the satisfaction of the ordering PSU. As far as party B is concerned, he was executing the job on behalf of party A but for the PSU, who placed the order and they were also successful in executing the order to the satisfaction of the ordering PSU. It is, therefore, the PSU issued successful completion certificate in favor of both the parties A & B, and as per your tendered eligibility criteria, both are eligible.

Case No. 26

You have invited bids for a project tender on an open tender basis. Five bids were received on the stipulated tender opening date and the same were opened in presence of bidders who wished to be present. After techno-commercial evaluation of the bids, three bids were found conforming to tender terms and conditions. Intimation about the price-bid opening was sent to techno-commercially qualified bidders for the opening of price bid on the stipulated date and time in presence of bidders. One of the techno-commercially eligible bidders has approached you with the request to allow him to withdraw his bid. What will be your stand in the case i.e. whether you will allow him to withdraw his bid or not.

Ans._____

_____

As the price bids have not been opened yet, you may accept the request of the bidder and allow him to withdraw his bid. Your decision shall be based primarily on the perception that even if you will not allow him to withdraw his bid if he emerged as the lowest bidder, he will run away. Thus, you will be wasting your time and energy on re-tendering besides waiting for the job to start.

Let's analyze the situation:

It sounds proper ethically but commercially the stand shall not be viable. Bidders are allowed to change their bids any number of times before the stipulated bid opening date and time. However, after the stipulated date and time of tender opening, it becomes legal and binding on both the parties to abide by the contractual terms and conditions of the tender.

As the bidder is contractually bound to fulfill his obligations under the tender, he shall not be allowed to withdraw his bid after the stipulated tender opening date and time, irrespective of the fact whether the techno-commercial evaluation is done or not.

As regards your perception that if this bidder who has requested for withdrawal of his bid turns out to be an L-1 bidder and backs out, as he has already requested for withdrawing his bid, your whole tendering process shall go in vain. However, please remember, as per the law of contract also, if has accepted your offer, he is liable to fulfill his commitment. Besides this, in that situation, you have stipulations in the terms of your tender documents regarding forfeiture of his Earnest Money deposit, Security Deposit, etc. or taking risk purchase action against the party.

Few public sector undertakings even decide for banning such bidder for a stipulated period if has backed out after emerging as Lowest Bidder. Nothing wrong with it as it works as a deterrent. However, keep in mind that such a decision can be taken only if the same is stipulated in tender terms and conditions. Terms and conditions of the tender are legal and binding on both the parties i.e. buyer and the bidder and not only on the bidder as perceived by many executives.

Case No. 27

You are the Marketing Head of your department and one of your responsibilities is to ensure timely home delivery of steel products to your customers. For this purpose, your office has entered into a transportation contract with a reputed contractor by inviting bids on an open tender basis. This contract is coming to an end in December 2017. Your office has recommended for extension of existing transportation contract for a period of three months i.e. Up to March 2018 as per the terms of the contract where it is stipulated that contract can be extended for a further period of three months on same rates, terms and conditions subject to satisfactory performance of the contract. The justification given by your office is that the contractor is placing vehicles as and when required without fail. Further, in the last quarter of the financial year, huge quantities have to be transported to government/public sector customers who have paid an advance for the material to be delivered to them. The file is put up to you for your approval, whether you will approve the extension or not. Please remember, as Marketing Head, it is your responsibility to boost sales and meet sales targets for the year.

Ans._____

Your answer obviously in this case shall be to approve the extension of the transportation contract. It appears correct and logical also keeping in view the fact that huge quantities have to be transported in the last quarter and this transporter knows the destination of most of your customers. Further, as per records, his performance is satisfactory as the transporter is placing trucks/trailers as per your requirement without fail.

Let's analyze the situation:

As explained above, decision making is primarily based on perception, and in the instant case, you and your office perceived the performance of the transporter as satisfactory based on the fact that he was always promptly placing trucks/trailers in your warehouse as and when required. Further, the sales targets were there in your mind and it was perceived by you that by continuing with the same transporter, the prompt deliveries to your customers shall be ensured. But have you ever thought whether satisfactory performance also means the material is reaching the customer and in time? Did you or your office check this fact before certifying his performance as satisfactory? Please look at the case given to you for taking the decision, it was mentioned that home delivery was required to be made to government/public sector customers who have made advance payments, thus whether they have received the material or not and in time has to be confirmed by them. When we are doing a post-mortem of the case, these things are drawing our attention but when we were making the decision to approve the extension, they never came to our mind. That's a big challenge in decision making.

This case-let is based on a real case where a decision was taken to approve the extension as it appeared the most prudent decision under the circumstances, when the transporter is selected on an open tender basis, he is promptly placing vehicles at your warehouse as per your instructions, during last quarter there is a pressure of meeting sales target and you don't want to take risk of non-delivery to your customers, etc. However, the transporter in this case was a big fraud. Instead of delivering material to customers and mainly to government customers, he was putting forged signature and stamp on the back of Goods Receipt and submitting it to your office. You neither had any procedure nor the infrastructure to check from customers whether they have received the material or not as the delivery point of such customers e.g. state electricity boards were in remote locations.

When this big fraud of crores of rupees was unearthed, the marketing head was also charge-sheeted by CBI in the case, only on the charge that he has not checked the satisfactory performance of the transporter without granting the extension. This case is very close to my heart again as the Marketing Head whom I am referring to is a friend of mine and he has been facing CBI wrath for more than two decades and has not got his promotions also although he was once the highest-rated executive of the Company.

Case No. 28

You are Project Manager of a big Company and your plant is being commissioned at full pace. Your operations people informed you that by installing few imported drives costing approximately Rs. 55lacs, Company shall save huge on energy costs during operation of the plant. You discussed with your senior management and they agreed. It was, however, informed that the project should not be delayed. The site engineer of the Indian distributor of the manufacturer company was incidentally at the site as they were awarded one package in the upcoming project.

You advised your operations people to expedite its procurement and raise indent for the same immediately. As it was a proprietary item being purchased for the first time, a budgetary quote was required from the overseas manufacturer as per the stipulated guidelines. To save time, your operation executives have sought your help in arranging the budgetary quote through a site engineer available at the site. Whether you will advise the site engineer to arrange a budgetary quote from the manufacturer and deliver by hand to expedite the procurement?

Ans._____

_____

A very simple case, Isn't it? Being Project Manager of the Company, you are keen to ensure completion of the project on time. Therefore, you will do this small favor to your operations, people, by arranging the budgetary quote through the site engineer of the manufacturer firms' distributor.

Let's analyze the decision.

In the purchase procedure of most of the public sector undertakings, it is stipulated that the budgetary quote for the proprietary item should be obtained directly from the manufacturer only. In the Manual for Procurement of Goods 2017 of the Government of India published by the Ministry of Finance, Department of Expenditure, it is stipulated that

"To the extent feasible, the firm may be asked to certify that the rates quoted by them are the same and not higher than those quoted with other Government, public sector, or private organizations."

It is further stipulated in the manual that the firm should be asked to accept a "Fall Clause" undertaking that, in case it supplies or quotes a lower rate to other Governments, public sector, or private organizations, it would reimburse the excess.

However, in the instant case, we have obtained a budgetary quote through the representative of the distributor who fudged the rates quoted by the original manufacturer as ascertained during the investigation of a case by CBI.

I keep on telling my participants that public sector executives, in general, are very nice people i.e. they think from the heart! Under normal circumstances, nobody can believe that a distributor or his representative will do this type of forgery and we endeavored to expedite the procurement which again was in the interest of the organization and not for any of our self motive.

However, CBI during the investigation has concluded that the laid down procedure of the Company was violated by the concerned officials with malafide intentions and recommended action for criminal conspiracy against the distributor, the indenter, his reporting officer, and also the head of the department.

Do you want to land yourself in this type of situation? If no, follow the procedure as it is written to keep you safe and secure because, under compelling circumstances, one is inclined to decide from his heart and not with the application of mind.

Case No. 29

You are procuring 10 different ceramic refractory items on a limited tender inquiry basis from five registered vendors. These vendors have been registered after following a due process. One party who was awarded an order for 4 ceramic refractory items failed to deliver the material in time even after repeated reminders. You were left with no other alternative but to initiate fresh tendering on his risk and cost. Now, you are going to place an inquiry for procuring 6 another ceramic refractory items, will you consider issuing an inquiry to this registered vendor who has failed to supply the material?

Ans._____

_____

Most probably, your answer shall be a big "NO". You are correct in your decision as he has failed to execute the earlier order and has put you to great inconvenience. Why he should be given the opportunity again?

Let's analyze your decision.

Generally, in a Public Sector Undertaking, we register the vendors/contractors after following a due process i.e. inviting applications from the interested vendors, scrutinizing them and inspecting the facilities offered, etc. and then register a party for sending inquiries to him for procurement on Limited Tender Enquiry basis.

In the instant case, it is perceived that due procedure was followed in registering this vendor for 10 different ceramic items. Due to some reason, he was not able to supply the 4 items ordered on him and you have gone for procuring the same on his risk and cost.

Your present enquiry is for 6 different items for which he is your registered vendor and he has not defaulted in the supply of these items. What will be your logic in refusing to send an enquiry to him except your perception that he may fail again? True, but can you make a decision based only on your perception. Will it be a prudent decision? Do you think in the case of a complaint by this vendor, investigating agencies shall also perceive the issue the way you have perceived? Do you want to land yourself into such a type of conflict? Your answer shall be no, therefore, you have to send an inquiry to him also for 6 items where he has not failed.

However, if you still feel that this party may not be able to supply you with these items also, please follow the stipulated procedure for banning business dealings with such parties. Believe me, there will be one in your organization also. Take action against the party as per the procedure, which in many cases, starts with the suspension of the party, as the banning proceedings may take a long time, with the approval of Competent Authority as per Delegation of Powers in your organization.

Case No. 30

You have floated a tender for the annual job contract in your plant. This job is being done through outsourcing for the last 10 years. The eligibility criteria stipulated in the tender is that the bidder should have successfully performed this job in any public sector during the last five years and the bidder has to submit a copy of the work order for the job executed. One of the bidders performed the job for your Organization twice in the last 5 years. However, in the first instance, he could successfully complete the job but in the subsequent tender although he was awarded the job being the lowest bidder, he could not complete the job and the contract was foreclosed but with no penalty to the contractor. He has applied against the fresh tender by submitting the work order for the year in which he performed the job successfully. Will you consider his bid?

Ans._____

_____

The first thought in your mind shall be to keep him away from the tendering process as he has failed to execute the job successfully in the last five years. It may also be brought to your notice that your company suffered a lot due to his inability to perform the job on time as envisaged. You will apprehend that in case he emerges as the lowest bidder, he may again run away after some time. Therefore, you shall decide to reject his bid.

Let's analyze the situation:

All this is correct but see the tender terms and conditions. Have you mentioned anywhere in the tender that parties who could not perform successfully in the last five years shall be disqualified? Whereas, you wanted a party who has executed the job even once successfully in the last five years which he did. Therefore, he is an eligible bidder as per stipulated tender eligibility criteria. Although, it is a fact that again awarding the job to the same party who failed once shall be a risky affair but this should have been decided at the time of framing tender terms and conditions. I am reiterating once again that any acceptance or rejection of a bid can be within stipulated criteria as mentioned in the tender terms and conditions.

Not convinced, go for re-tendering. Who stops you, as you have not yet opened the price-bids and you have a valid reason for fresh tendering. However, this time specifically stipulating in the tender terms that party who was unsuccessful in executing a similar job during the last five years shall not be considered.

Now that you have tried taking decisions under so many complex situations, don't you agree that in many decisions you took, they were influenced by your emotions? It is a fact that we have trained our mind to analyze the situation emotionally as most of the decisions we take in our day-to-day lives are concerning the persons we are emotionally attached to e.g. husband/wife, kids, relatives, friends, and other acquaintances, etc. Therefore, while taking a decision, we listen to our hearts, whereas, in professional decision making we are required to listen to our minds.

Not agreeing, try out the following decision-making exercise, where I have given you four alternatives and you have to select the best one under the given situation.

CHAPTER 16

Decision Making in PSE – MCQ Exercise

"Learn from others' mistakes, you can't live long enough to make them all yourself"

— Chanakya

1. As head of projects of your plant, you have envisaged a problem in completing a project in time due to the non-availability of one critical imported item which is proprietary. Site Engineer of his Indian distributor is working at your site. To ensure timely completion of the project and to expedite preparing indent on priority, you will:

   a. Advise your department to raise emergency indent.

   b. Advise your department to seek a budgetary quote through the site engineer of the manufacturer's as he will arrange the same immediately.

   c. Advice your department to seek a budgetary quote from the Indian distributor as the manufacturer will take a very long time to respond and you can't wait.

   d. Advise your department to seek a budgetary quote from the manufacturer.

2. Your Company has invited bids from 3 reputed manufacturers on Limited Tender Enquiry (LTE) basis for procuring 1500 MT special steel Slabs on an immediate delivery basis as your sister plant who was catering you the semis is down and customers are insisting for timely deliveries. The L-1 rate received is Rs. 73000/- pmt, L-2 is Rs. 75000/- pmt and L-3 is Rs. 76000/- pmt whereas your internal estimated price was Rs. 70000/- pmt. Due to urgency, MM Department requested the L-1 party to reduce the prices through the mail but the party refused. However, after repeated requests and persuasion over the phone and through emails they agreed to reduce the price to Rs. 72000/- pmt. The purchase department has now sent you the file for justifying the reasonability of the L-1 rates. As HOD of indenting department, you will:

   a. Justify the reasonability of rates and recommend procurement because of urgency.
   b. Not accept the rates and advise for re-tendering.
   c. Advice for negotiation with L-1 bidder by the committee
   d. Revise the estimate and justify the reasonability of L-1 rates because of an emergency.

3. Your Company has invited bids for civil work with financial eligibility criteria of successful completion of one work amounting to Rs. 5 crores and above during the last three years as per tender conditions. During the techno-commercial evaluation, it was observed that one bidder has submitted a copy of the work order amounting to Rs. 6 crores for successfully completing such a job for another PSU in a single work order along with the completion certificate. It was, however, observed that material i.e. Steel and Cement amounting to Rs. 2.50 crores was supplied by the PSU free of cost to the bidder as was found mentioned in the work order. As head of the evaluation committee, you will:

a. Accept his bid
b. Reject his bid
c. Ask him to provide details of work done
d. Seek the advice of your superior in the matter.

4. You are HOD of your department and one of the techno-commercially eligible bidders has approached you with the request to allow him to withdraw his bid against the tender floated for your department. You will:
   a. Allow withdrawal of the bid
   b. Not allow withdrawal of the bid
   c. Allow withdrawal with forfeiture of EMD
   d. Allow withdrawal of bid with the condition that he will not be considered in case of re-tendering of the same case.

5. Your department has awarded a transportation contract for transporting steel materials on an open tender basis for six months which is ending on 31st December 2017 with a clause that the contract can be extended for a further period of 3 months on mutual consent subject to satisfactory performance of the transporter. The transporter has been regularly placing the trucks/trailers as per your requirements. A proposal has been moved by your office in November 2017 to approve an extension for a further period of three months as huge quantities have to be transported during the period as the financial year is ending and the new contractor may not be able to perform efficiently and also mentioned in the proposal that performance of the current transporter is satisfactory. You are also under severe pressure to ensure delivery to customers within March 2018. As approving authority, you will:

a. Approve the extension.

b. Not approve the extension.

c. Advise your department to justify the satisfactory performance of the transporter.

d. Advise your department to enter into an emergency contract for 3 months to ensure expeditious transportation of balance material within March 2018.

6. Your Company has floated a tender for certain jobs to be outsourced in a critical area of the plant. The tender specifications and eligibility criteria were kept as suggested by the Indenter. After techno-commercial evaluation, 4 out of 5 bidders were found meeting required eligibility criteria and price bids of eligible bidders were opened. The file was sent to the Indenting Department for justifying the reasonability of L-1 rates. Although, rates were found reasonable but it was informed by the Indenter that the L-1 party may not be able to perform satisfactorily citing an example of a different outsourcing job where the party could not perform thus resulting in a huge loss of production and has advised for rejecting his bid. You are Head of Operations of your plant and the file is pending with you for approval. You will:

    a. Advice for rejecting the bid of the party based on information received from the executing authority and go ahead with the tendering process.

    b. Advise re-tendering in the case with revised specifications

    c. Seek written report from the executing authority (indenter) on his poor performance and reject the bid.

    d. Approve to award the job to the lowest bidder.

7. In the case of a project tender floated by you, bids by consortium members are also allowed. It was mentioned in the tender terms

that eligible bidders shall be allowed to change the constitution and composition of the consortium. Bids have been opened and techno-commercial evaluation is on. A bidder has approached you with the request to allow the change in the composition of the consortium. You will:

a. Allow change in the composition of the consortium.

b. Not allow a change in the composition of the consortium.

c. Advise them to wait till the techno-commercial evaluation is over.

d. Reject their bid as the new consortium may not be able to execute the job.

8. You are floating enquiry for procurement of Heavy Duty Motor for your department on LTE basis to four registered manufacturers. In the meantime, one local dealer approached you for giving enquiries to two reputed manufacturers of this type of motor. Will you issue an inquiry to these two parties also to increase competition and to get the best price for your procurement?

a. Yes

b. Yes, with Provisional Registration

c. Yes, if the manufacturers can establish their credentials

d. No

9. You have finalized the tender for the rebuilding of coke over batteries valuing Rs. 110 crores in six months from the date of tendering. However, L-1 backs out after the award of the contract stating that his bid has expired yesterday. L-2 (a renowned contractor) has offered to do the job at L-1 rates and on the same terms and conditions. Your project is suffering badly due to an inordinate delay in the finalization of the tender. As recommending authority, you will recommend:

a. For the award of the job to L-2 at L-1 rates.

b. Negotiations with L-2 as he has become L-1 after the withdrawal of bid by L-1 bidder.

c. Cancel the tender and go for fresh tendering

d. Award the job to L-2 and advice for banning of L-1 bidder.

10. In the above case, if it is decided to go for re-tendering in the case, whether you will:

    a. Allow L-1 bidder (who backed out) in the re-tendering

    b. You will not allow him (L-1 bidder) in the re-tendering

    c. You will allow him if he gives an undertaking that he will not back out again

    d. You will not allow him and rather recommend banning of this bidder in any other tendering also for six months.

11. You are Head of Finance of Your Unit. A file has been received for your concurrence before approval of Chief Executive for procurement of 20000 MT Charcoal tendered on an open tender basis and rates finalized after protracted negotiations. The technical specifications beside others are that Charcoal supplied should be with a minimum of 70% Carbon and a maximum of 10% moisture. You observed that one party who offered Charcoal with minimum 75% Carbon and maximum 5% moisture has emerged L-2 and the difference between rates of L-1 & L-2 is only Rs. 150/- pmt i.e. you will be getting 10% extra charcoal (Carbon) if the tender is awarded to L-2 bidder i.e. huge savings to your plant. You will:

    a. Advise procurement from L-2 bidder because of huge savings.

    b. Advice for re-tendering with revised specifications including provision for bonus/penalties.

    c. Give concurrence to the proposal for procurement from L-1 bidder.

    d. Advice re-negotiations with the (L-1) lowest bidder

12. In a tender for consultancy contract with an estimated value of Rs. 1.00 Crores (estimate based on the budgetary quote from one of the bidders), 4 best consultants in the country were found eligible and the price was discovered through Reverse Auction (RA) where 85 times bidding was found done. L-1 was at Rs. 20 Lacs (incidentally the party who gave budgetary quote), L-2 was Rs. 23 lacs, L-3 was Rs. 27 lacs, and L-4 was Rs. 31 lacs. As approving authority, you will:

    a. Advise re-tendering in the case
    b. Advice fresh tender with a revised estimate
    c. Approve for placement of an order on L-1
    d. Advice banning of business dealings with the party who gave an exaggerated budgetary quote.

13. A critical bearing in your plant suddenly broke and production came to stand-still resulting in a daily production loss of Rs. 5 crores per day approximately. This is a special type of bearing and not available in the plant. The next day, Purchase Department could find a dealer who has the required bearing and offered it at Rs. 2.00 crores (non-negotiable) whereas the Last Purchase Price of this bearing was Rs. 85 Lacs only. As Head of Purchase Department, you will:

    a. Approve to procure the bearing at Rs. 2.00 crores.
    b. Not approved to procure the same at this exorbitant price.
    c. You will advise the department to negotiate with the dealer
    d. You will advise for short-term tendering.

14. Your daughter is employed in the Consultancy firm who has also applied for the award of financial consultancy contract against the tender floated by your Company (although no way related to the type of work for which tender is floated). You, as Finance Head of the Company, are required to evaluate the bids received. Whether you will

a. Evaluate the bids as it is your job.

b. Reject his bid as it may result in a conflict of interest.

c. Inform your superior and stay away from the evaluation process.

d. You will evaluate the bids under intimation to your superior.

15. You are regularly procuring 10 different ceramic refractory items on a limited tender enquiry basis from five registered vendors. These vendors have been registered after following a due process. One of these registered vendors on whom the order was placed for 4 ceramic refractory items failed to deliver these items in time stating some technical reasons and has asked for more time to supply. In the meantime, you have received an indent (purchase requisition) for procuring 5 other ceramic refractory items. As head of the Purchase Department, you will:

a. Advice for sending an enquiry to only four registered vendors i.e. excluding the defaulting vendor.

b. Advise banning action against the defaulting vendor

c. Advise canceling the registration of the defaulting vendor

d. Advise sending an enquiry to all the five registered vendors.

16. As Head of Marketing of your Division, you are worried about poor sales during the year and large inventory build-up in your warehouse and the financial year is coming to an end. One customer approaches you for purchasing the material which is lying in inventory for the last ten months. The deal is finalized at Rs. 5 crores and he submits a Letter of Credit (L/C) on 30th March 2018. You forwarded the L/C to your Finance Manager. He informed that the L/C appears to be in order but as per stipulated guidelines, the L/C has to be got verified by issuing as well as controlling bank. However, it is late evening on 30th March and all you could do is send your senior executive to the issuing branch for verification. He brought the written confirmation letter from the Branch Manager of the issuing Bank. On 31st March,

banks are closed for annual closing. Therefore, confirmation from Controlling Bank is not possible. Since the sales are very poor this year and this deal is for your old non-moving stock at discounted rates which are valid up to 31st March only, whether, you will:

a. Advise Finance for issuance of Delivery Order

b. Advise Finance Manager to re-confirm from issuing bank himself and then issue Delivery Order.

c. As per your experience, obtaining confirmation from the controlling office is a mere formality, therefore you will advise finance in writing to issue a delivery order.

d. Advise Finance to do the needful in the matter even if you forgo sales.

17. You have floated a tender for the annual job contract in your plant. This job is being done through outsourcing for the last many years. The eligibility criteria stipulated in the tender is that the bidder should have successfully performed this job in any PSE during the last five years and the bidder was required to submit a copy of the work order for the job executed along with a successful completion certificate. During the evaluation of the bids, it was observed that one of the bidders who performed this job for your Organization twice in the last 5 years has also quoted with required documents. However, in the first instance, he could successfully complete the job but in the subsequent tender awarded to him, he could not complete the job and the contract was foreclosed. He has applied against the fresh tender by submitting the work order for the year in which he performed the job successfully along with a successful completion certificate. Will you…

a. Accept his bid

b. Reject his bid

c. Ask the party to submit all the work orders.

d. Reject his bid and initiate banning action against the party to avoid such recurrences in the future.

18. Against your indent for procuring 150 bearings urgently (to be delivered within 30 days from PO) as they are required for capital repairs, MM Department informed that although all the ten registered parties have submitted quote but only 3 have agreed to supply the bearings in 45 days from the date of order, 3 have asked for 60 days and balance 4 parties have asked for 90 days delivery period despite repeated requests. They have sought your written advice on the delivery period to be agreed as price-bids of only those parties will be opened who are within the delivery period agreed by the indenter. What will be your decision concerning the delivery period in the case?

    a. You will allow parties who quoted a delivery period of 45 days.

    b. You will allow parties who quoted a delivery period of 60 days.

    c. You will allow parties who quoted a delivery period of 90 days.

    d. You will advise for re-tendering the case with a revised delivery period.

19. In the above case, after seeking written confirmation from Indenter, you opened a price-bid of only 3 parties out of 10 bids received for those who have offered to deliver bearings within 45 days, and the following rates were found quoted.

    i. Party A – Rs. 12000/- each for 50 bearings for immediate delivery (ex-stock) and Rs. 12500/- each for balance 100 bearings.

    ii. Party B – Rs. 12200/- each for 150 bearings for delivery within 45 days

    iii. Party C – Rs. 13000/- each for 150 bearings for delivery within 45 days.

    However, immediately after the opening of price-bids, party A has given in writing to voluntarily reduce his rates as Rs. 12,000/- each for all the 150 bearings. Please rank the party as L-1, L-2 & L-3.

a. Party A – L-1 @ Rs. 12,000/- for 150 bearings
b. Party B – L-1 for 150 bearings
c. Party A, L-1 for 50 bearings and party B, L-1 for balance 100 bearings.
d. You will reject Party A's offer being conditional.

20. You have awarded a contract amounting to Rs. 20 crores for Scientific Exploitation of coal at your collieries to L-1 bidder for two years from the date of Letter of Intent (LOI). As per the tender terms, the successful bidder was required to submit a security deposit (SD) of Rs. 50 lacs in the form of Demand Draft/Pay Order/Bank Guarantee within 15 days from the award of LOI. The contractor is working in your collieries in other areas also and his bills for more than Rs. 1 crore is pending for payment in your office. He has requested you to adjust the security deposit from his pending bills. What will be your stand in the case?

    a. You will insist on payment of SD as stipulated in tender terms
    b. You will accept his request for adjustment of SD from pending bills
    c. You will cancel the EOI and forfeit EMD if he fails to deposit SD within a stipulated time.
    d. You will refer the matter to the Law Department for their advice on the matter.

21. Your company has floated a tender for the award of Handling Contract with an estimated value of Rs. 10 crore p.a. for 4 years duration for one of the warehouses. Bidders are required to possess at least 10 cranes of different capacity either in the name of the company, director, partner, or proprietor. As per tender conditions, techno-commercially eligible bidders shall be required to show original documents for cranes owned by them as mentioned in their

tender documents as and when asked by the Tender Committee. You received 7 bids but during techno-commercial evaluation only 4 bidders viz. A, B, C & D were found eligible. It was observed during checking/scrutiny of documents that two parties (let's say A and C) have submitted an identical list of equipment owned by them in their tender documents, however, both were meeting the condition of ownership as stipulated in the tender terms. Tender Committee requested all the four eligible bidders to produce original documents for verification. Only three parties (A, B & D) presented the original documents for verification as stipulated in the tender conditions and the original documents were also found in order. However, party C is not producing the original documents for verification despite repeated reminders. You will:

a. Reject bid of the party C as per stipulated tender terms

b. You will accept the bid of the party C

c. You will give party C a final chance to produce documents within the stipulated date and if he fails, you will reject his bid

d. You will go for re-tendering to invite more competition.

22. You have floated a tender for the award of conversion contract for two years for converting your semis (Billets) to Bars (TMT) 18 to 22mm size. It is mentioned in the tender that the facilities offered by the bidder shall be thoroughly inspected before the award of the contract. TEC decided to inspect a rolling of 22 mm TMT as 22mm is a non-standard size and difficult to the role. Further, 22mm TMT is used for roof-bolting of underground mines that's why it is very critical. Out of 3 eligible bidders, 2 have agreed to get the rolling of 22mm TMT inspected but one party (X) is insisting on inspection of rolling of 18 or 20mm TMT as they do not have any orders for 22mm TMT and it will add to their inventory. All your efforts to convince them have failed. You will:

a. Reject the bid of party X
b. Accept the bid of party X
c. Insist party X for inspection of 22mm TMT rolling and keep tender in abeyance.
d. Go for fresh tendering in the case.

23. You are Head of Personnel of a small plant with around 800 workers. Due to an inordinate delay in the supply of uniforms to workers, they have threatened to go on strike if the same is not supplied immediately. Your Chief Executive has asked you to arrange the uniforms urgently to avoid any IR problem. You are aware that procuring uniforms through the Purchase Department will take time. You believe that as this is a simple case of purchase and your department is capable of handling this procurement. How will you proceed with procurement?

    a. You will advise your Department for procurement.
    b. You will advise for emergency procurement because of the IR problem and to avoid a strike by workers.
    c. You will advise your department to seek approval of the Chief Executive for a single tender (non-proprietary) purchase and to procure from the best supplier.
    d. You will advise the Purchase Department for expeditious procurement.

24. You are Chief Executive of a plant producing Ferro Manganese. Over the past few years, you are running your plant at 70% of rated capacity due to sluggish market and tied up for your raw material requirement with a reputed supplier on a long term Memorandum of Understanding (MoU) for the supply of 70000 MT raw material per annum which was sufficient to meet your production targets. Due to a sudden surge in demand, your customers are asking for more material. You have therefore decided to increase production at

your plant but you are not having raw material to meet the increased production target. Your MoU supplier has expressed his inability to supply you with more than the contracted quantity.

One of your known producers informed that he has imported the Ferro Manganese and the same is reaching Indian Port in a day. He also agreed to give your plant, 10000 MT from his consignment and on the rates you are paying to your regular supplier. However, he asked for Purchase Order within 24 hours to avoid port charges. In the instant case, whether, you will:

a. Advise the Purchase Department to immediately place Purchase Order and seek post-facto approval.

b. Advice Operations department to raise emergency indent to ensure immediate procurement.

c. Advice Purchase Department for expeditious procurement.

d. Request the party to increase the time for placing the Purchase Order.

25. You are Project Manager of your Company and in the on-going modernization work in your plant; the contractor sought a time extension to complete the job stating that he could not complete the work in time as there was inordinate delay in handing over the site to him by the plant authorities, which was a fact. Further, a considerable delay was observed in handing over the drawings/designs, etc. to the contractor. However, you are aware that there were delays from the contractor's side also in arranging man/material/machinery from his side. You are also aware, that any dispute at this stage regarding the imposition of penalty/LD may result in further delaying the project and the contractor may stop the work if you impose a penalty, which you cannot afford at this juncture. What will be your further course of action on the matter?

a. You will allow the contractor to complete the work keeping the issue of delay analysis in abeyance to ensure continuity.

b. You will allow the contractor to complete the work only after the finalization of the delay analysis.

c. You will allow the contractor to complete the work only after the finalization of the amount recoverable towards LD, if any.

d. You will allow the contractor to complete the work without prejudice to your rights to impose a penalty at a later date.

26. Your Company has invited bids for underground cabling work in your Plant. The cables were required to be of particular 'brand'. The only other eligibility criteria were that the bidder should have successfully executed this job in any other PSE and must submit the letter on the letterhead of the PSE confirming the successful execution of the job. 4 bids were received against the above tender and tender committee during evaluation observed that all the 4 bidders have submitted the original experience certificate. Tender Committee will:

a. Request Purchase/Contract Department to seek confirmation from issuing PSEs.

b. Request your Vigilance Department to verify genuineness.

c. Ask bidders to submit confirmation from PSEs about the issuance of experience certificate.

d. Declare all the bidders eligible based on original certificates submitted by them.

27. As Chief Executive of your Plant, you have received a report from your vigilance department that the party who is doing the underground electrical cabling work at your plant has grabbed the order based on a forged experience certificate. However, as the order was placed on the party around four months ago, more than 70% job has been successfully completed by the party, and the cable supplied is found

acceptable and matching with IS specifications by your inspection department. What will be your next course of action?

a. Immediately order for stoppage of work by the party.

b. Immediately order for stoppage of work and black-listing of the party.

c. Ask your Contract Department to foreclose the contract and go for risk-purchase action for the balance work.

d. Allow the party to continue the work but initiate criminal action against the party.

28. You are Head of the Tender Committee for evaluation of 5 bids received for civil work in hot zone area of your plant with one of the eligibility criteria that bidder should have successfully executed the same/similar job in any PSE during last 3 years. Two bidders A and B have submitted an experience certificate from a reputed PSE for successfully completing the required job. It was observed that party B was a sub-contractor to party 'A' and he actually executed the job at that PSE. However, both have submitted the experience certificate for the same job duly signed on the letterhead of the PSE. All other terms and conditions are fulfilled by both parties. What will be your decision in the case concerning acceptance/rejection of their bids?

a. You will accept the bid of party A as he was awarded the job by the PSE and reject the bid of the party B as he was a sub-contractor.

b. You will accept the bid of party B as he has successfully executed the job and reject the bid of party A as he has not actually executed the job.

c. You will reject bids of both parties A & B as party A, who received the order from PSE never performed the job, and party B as he has received the order from party A who is a private party.

d. You will accept bids of both parties A & B.

29. As Planning Cell In-charge, you are raising indent for procurement of one ABC pump for your new unit out of the two pumps which were installed by the supplier during the commissioning of the plant as the same is giving trouble. These pumps are critical for production. Considering the compatibility, reliable operation, and criticality of these pumps, you will raise indent on:
    a. M/s. ABC Pumps on a Proprietary basis
    b. Raise emergency indent because of the criticality
    c. Issue Limited Tender Enquiry on reputed suppliers mentioning technical specifications
    d. Issue Open Tender for procurement giving detailed specifications, terms, and conditions, etc.

30. Price-bids of the bidders who were found techno-commercially eligible were opened on the stipulated date and time in presence of bidders. Party ABC Ltd. was found the lowest bidder followed by the party XYZ Ltd. as the L-2 bidder. However, after the opening of price-bids, M/s. XYZ complained that ABC Ltd. has never done the job envisaged in this tender and they have submitted the forged certificate. Upon inquiry, it was found that the experience certificate was submitted by M/s. ABC Ltd. was forged. What will be your further course of action? You will:
    a. Reject his bid and re-tender the case
    b. Reject his bid and go ahead with the tendering process
    c. Initiate banning/criminal action against party ABC and go ahead with the tendering process.
    d. Contemplate criminal proceedings against party ABC and go for fresh tendering.

Answers: 1(a), 2(c), 3(b), 4(b), 5(c), 6(d), 7(c), 8(d), 9(c), 10(a), 11(c), 12(c), 13(a), 14(c), 15(d) 16(d), 17(a), 18(d), 19(b), 20(b), 21(b), 22(b), 23(d), 24(c), 25(c), 26(a), 27(d), 28(d), 29(d), 30(c).

www.ingramcontent.com/pod-product-compliance
Lightning Source LLC
Chambersburg PA
CBHW020906180526
45163CB00007B/2646